The Golden Age of the
CIRCUS

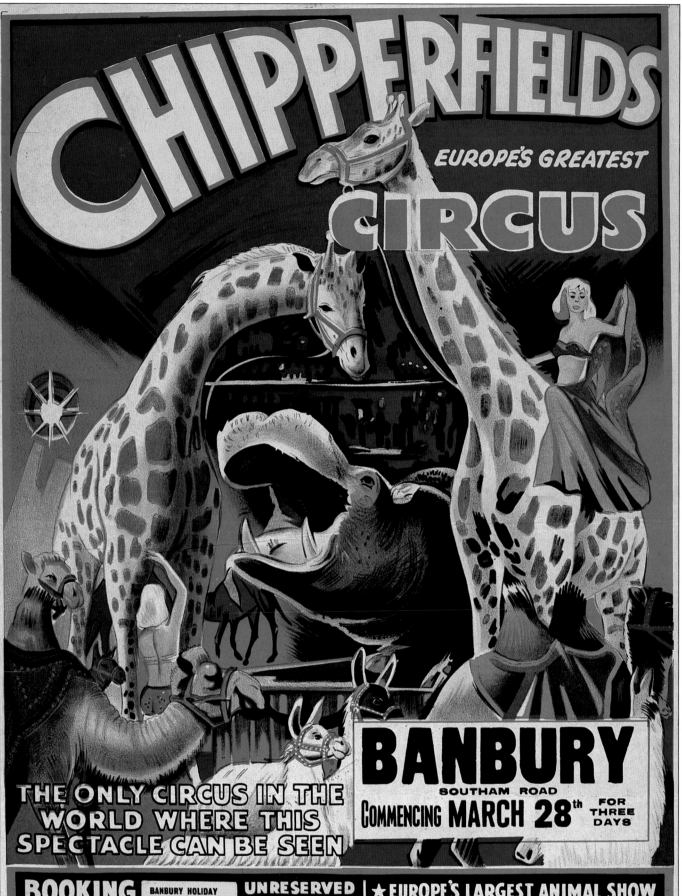

The Golden Age of the
CIRCUS

Howard Loxton
Circus Consultant: David Jamieson

SMITHMARK

This edition published in 1997 by Smithmark Publishers, a division of U.S. Media Holdings, Inc., 16 East 32nd Street, New York, NY 10016.

SMITHMARK books are available for bulk purchase for sales promotion and premium use. For details write or call the manager of special sales, SMITHMARK Publishers, 16 East 32nd Street, New York, NY 10016; (212) 532-6600.

Produced by **Regency House Publishing Limited**
The Grange, Grange Yard, London SE1 3AG

ISBN 0-765-199092

Printed in China

10 9 8 7 6 5 4 3 2 1

TITLE PAGES

Left: The Chipperfields are a remarkable family of animal trainers as well as circus proprietors. This poster was used in the late 1950s, and early 1960s.

Right: The Tony Alexis Trio, three clowns who worked together with great timing and an infectious sense of fun.

ABOVE: Circus Parade c.1891.

FRONT COVER: Part of a 1920s poster for Ringling Brothers and Barnum and Bailey Combined Shows.

BACK COVER: TOP – 1914 poster advertising two Chinese troupes appearing with the Barnum and Bailey Circus.

BELOW – Poster for an equestrian revue at the Nouveau Cirque in Paris 1889.

Acknowledgements

Any book such as this owes a great debt to former writers on the subject. To their chagrin enthusiasts excited at finding some interesting 'new' information will usually find that authors such as Earl Chapin May (The Circus from Rome to Ringling, revised 1963), George L. Chindhal (A History of the Circus in America, 1959), Henry Thétard (La Merveilleuse Histoire du Cirque, 1947, 1978) and George Speaight (A History of the Circus, 1980) have been there before them. Those interested in circus history will find Speaight's bibliography a useful guide to circus sources while the dedicated student should consult R. Toole Stott's Circus and Allied Arts – A World Bibliography. More recent general books on American circus include Wilton Eckley's The American Circus (1984) and LaVahn G. Hoh and William H. Rough's Step Right Up! (1990) both very readable and with bibliographies.

The author would particularly like to thank Mr David Jamieson, editor of King Pole, published by the Circus Friends Association, former President of the C.F.A. and himself the author of several circus books, for reading and commenting on the text as well as supplying many of the photographs and other illustrations. His information and advice have been invaluable. The author is indebted to the librarians of the British Library and the Theatre Museum, London and would also like to thank his picture researcher Mrs Diana Phillips for her contribution, Neil Grant for editing the text and Annabel Trodd for the lively design of the book.

The publishers thank those circuses, institutions and individuals who have supplied illustrations or permitted reproduction of material which is their copyright and thank Ringling Brothers and Barnum and Bailey Combined Shows Inc. for permission to reproduce advertising material involving circus names they own. These names are: Ringling Bros. and Barnum and Bailey Circus; Barnum & Bailey Greatest Show on Earth; Ringling Bros. World's Greatest Shows; Sells-Floto Circus; Hagenbeck-Wallace Circus; Sparks Circus; Al G. Barnes Circus; Forepaugh-Sells Bros. Circus; John Robinson Circus. Other individual credits as follows: Archaos – Cirque de caractère 108r; Big Apple Circus 110t,110b; Philip Gandey/Chinese State Circus 99r; Alexis Gruss Circus 107t; Circus Knie 46b,46t,70-1b (based with permission on original artwork © Ringling Brothers Barnum and Bailey),102-3; Le Cercle Invisible 108l; Circus Friends Association of Great Britain Archives 6l,37,66b,77t. Clyde Beatty-Cole Brothers Circus 104; David and Janice Davis 33tr,cr,br,frt. Dover Publications (from Old Time Circus Cuts) 12b,32t,40t,49,52b,96br,99tl; Mr David Jamieson 3,6,8-9,12t,17t, 36-7,38-9,40-1,41,43,45t,46-7,47b,50,52tl,tr,53tl,tr,54tr, 55tl,tr,b,57tl,tr,c,br,59(3), 61(2),63,65l,67,68, 69r, 71t,b,72,73tr,br,79tr,b,81l,r,82t,83,86t,b,88,89,93b,94t,b,95t,96t,bl,97b,101bl, br,105, 106-7,107r,111t,b; David Jamieson Collection 2,6-7(2),29,35b,39,56br,65r,79tl,80l,r,82b,85,87, 107l,109. Mander and Mitchenson Theatre Collection 10t,11t,18b,23; Mansell Collection 15,42b; Mr George Speaight 62t. Geoff Stevens Collection 85l. All other illustrations are from the Library of Congress and private collections.

Contents

CLOCKWISE

Ringling Brothers Circus (Red Unit) on tour in 1985. There is a motorcycle globe of death set up in the far end ring, and animal trainer Gunther Gebel-Williams is on the back of an African elephant coming down the track as the company presents the finale of the show.

A 1970s programme for the German Circus Busch.

Programme for the Bouglione Circus, from the early 1960s. This French circus operated on tour and at both the Cirque d'Hiver and the Medrano buildings in Paris.

A Poster from the late 1950s for Sir Robert Fossett's Circus.

Introduction

'The Greatest Show on Earth!' That's what P.T. Barnum called the circus. He meant his own circus, of course, and Barnum was the greatest ever exponent of ticket-selling hype, but it is true. The circus, in all its variety, surely is the greatest show on earth. Where else can you experience physical thrills, music, dance, pathos, slapstick, subtle humour, sleight-of-hand, amazing feats, acrobatic skills, fine horsemanship, not to mention performing animals and in former times at least, human 'freaks'? And all in one show, with perhaps a knife thrower, a Shakespearean soliloquy or a re-creation of an ancient Roman chariot race thrown in. You may not see all those acts in the circuses of today but you will see an enormously varied entertainment of skills and showmanship, thrills and laughter, chutzpah and charivari that nothing else can offer.

There have been many changes in recent years, brought about by economics, changing attitudes to animals and the competition of electronic entertainments. Indeed, you can watch circus on television, but to experience it properly you need to be sitting by the ring, knowing that the performers are doing this for you, seeing the bright lights turn tinsel into glittering gold, feeling the other spectators hold their breath, smelling the sawdust (and the sweat) and maybe letting the clown make a fool of you. Nothing can take the place of being there, no film or video, nor indeed a book. Nevertheless, we hope to capture here something of the circus atmosphere, to recount its history and celebrate some of its great performers – human and animal. So watch the parade and roll up to the big top for the show. We guarantee a ringside seat.

ONE
History of the Circus

Circus is part of the long history of entertainment, but the circus as we know it today is little more than two centuries old. When and where was that mixture of acts, performed within a circular arena which could be recognized as circus, first performed? Most historians would agree that the place was London in the 1760s. Since then circuses have flourished, failed and flourished again all around the world.

In the Roman arena in Nîmes, France, the liberty horses of the Cirque Arlette Gruss are put through their paces at rehearsal. A modern circus performs inside an ancient one where men and animals performed nearly 2,000 years ago.

Origins of the Circus

The word circus means a circle in Latin. It is given to circular street junctions like Columbus Circle in New York or Piccadilly Circus in London, or to a ring of elegant houses like those built in 18th-century Bath, when that English spa was becoming a fashionable resort for the upper classes. More than a century before that, it was applied to a riding ring where gentlemen exercised their horses in the middle of London's Hyde Park, and in classical times the Romans called their race tracks circuses. The most famous was the Circus Maximus, a great arena at the foot of the Palatine Hill in Rome where horse races and other events were held. Actually it was not round but oval, but the races went round and round. Some people look back to that as the beginning of the circus, but what went on there was not much like what we think of as a circus performance today.

Many of the kinds of acts and performers, human and animal, which we now associate with circus were indeed part of the entertainment of Roman times and earlier. The ancient Egyptians had skilled animal trainers, and acrobatic feats still seen today appear in early Chinese carvings. However, the Roman Circus was for horse and chariot racing and though the Colosseum in Rome and the arenas in other cities throughout the Roman Empire were circular or oval, the crowds attending their bloodthirsty 'entertainments' were more interested in seeing wild animals attacking Christians and criminals, or gladiators engaged in often fatal duels, than in marvelling at how well they were trained. Acrobats and performing animals were more likely to be seen as separate acts in market places or at private parties.

Through the succeeding centuries, strongmen, rope dancers, tumblers and jugglers, dancing dogs and bears were among the itinerant entertainers who travelled from town to town and fair to fair displaying the skills which still amaze us. Many of the famous circus families are descended from them. The British Chipperfields, for instance, claim to trace their roots back to a showman who presented a performing bear at the Frost Fair held in London on the frozen River Thames in 1684. The Ravels, one of whom took on the great wire-walker Blondin as an apprentice, could trace their line back to rope dancers in 1603. The Wallendas, the Knies, the Fossetts and many more had been performers for generations – but the kind of shows these people gave did not constitute a circus until the middle of the 18th century. It was then that the elements were brought together which offered a variety of different acts, including horsemanship, trained animals, acrobats and clowns, presented in a mixed show and in a circular performance area – a circus.

The person generally credited with doing this for the first time, though he did not use the name circus, was an Englishman called Philip Astley. The place, Halfpenny Hatch in London, was a patch of ground on the south bank of the River Thames not far from the modern rail terminal of Waterloo Station. The site, identified by ringmaster and

A contemporary portrait of Philip Astley.

A Danish bill advertising a troupe of tumblers and leapers in 1749. They are presented by a clown in harlequin dress.

circus manager Chris Barltrop, is now marked by an inn called the White Hart, on the corner of Cornwall Road and Roupel Street. Close by is the National Theatre and a little downstream is Bankside, the entertainment area of Elizabethan London where bear-baiting pits and Shakespeare's theatre stood.

Astley, the son of a cabinetmaker, was born in 1742 in Newcastle-under-Lyme, a pottery town in the middle of England. He was put to work at his father's trade but his own interests centred on horses and riding. At 17, after a blazing row with his father, he left home. At Coventry he enlisted in the army and became a breaker-in of horses. He already commanded considerable horsemanship and according to one account his fellow soldiers were amazed to see him standing on the back of a galloping horse, jumping on and off its back and even balancing on his head as the horse cantered round and round. He fought in Germany during the Seven Years War (1756-63), distinguishing himself in action by capturing a standard from the French and then rescuing the Duke of Brunswick, who had charged through the enemy lines and become unhorsed. Back in Britain, having risen to the rank of sergeant-major, he was presented to King George II.

Having heard of other horsemen setting up as riding masters and making money by giving displays of horsemanship, Astley sought his discharge from the army, which was granted along with a gift from his commanding officer of a splendid white charger. He made his way to London, met a fine horsewoman, married her, and bought an intelligent little horse called Billy, the first of several. He staked a claim to a piece of ground not far from Lambeth Bridge and roped out a circuit in which to give displays. Each afternoon he mounted his charger at the southern end of the bridge and handed out bills announcing his performance, pointing the way downstream with his sword to direct people to where the performance would take place.

His friend Jacob Decastro, whose memoirs (1824) include an account of Astley's career, described how he earlier had got a post as a groom at Sampson's Riding School, where part of his job was to parade the streets with a trumpet to advertise his employer's riding display. He studied Sampson's methods of teaching, breaking horses and riding tricks. But neither he nor Sampson, an ex-cavalryman, was the first to exhibit horsemanship in London. That was probably an Irishman called Thomas Jackson who, in1758, would ride standing astride the saddles of two horses with a third between them. Thomas Price, whose family later became prominent among circus folk, was giving shows up and down the country before exhibiting in London in 1767. His display included jumping two horses over a bar while he stood astride them and picking a whip from the ground at full gallop. Another pioneer was Jacob Bates, who had already been to Russia, given displays in Germany, the Netherlands and France, and was soon to take his exhibition to America. He amazed spectators by riding while standing on the

On full speed between 2 Horses resting only on his Arms

Leaping a Bar standing upon 2 Horses with one foot on each Saddle on full speed

Jumping as He rides 2 Horses on full speed

Takes his Whip from the Ground on full speed

Riding upon His Head and fireing a Pistol on full speed

Standing with one Leg on the Saddle on full speed

Laying across 3 Horses on full speed

Riding backwards standing on the Saddle on full speed

An engraving for the Universal Museum and Complete Magazine showing the trick riding of Thomas Price in 1767.

LEFT
Tumblers, a rope dancer and a performing bear in the Fechthaus in Nuremberg, Germany, in the late 17th century. Here plays and bull-baiting also took place in a structure which, like the theatres of Shakespeare's London, combined elements of the inn yard and the trestle stage.

inside stirrups of two horses, by standing on the saddle and controlling four, by leaping on and off horses at full gallop, by vaulting over a horse from side to side, and by reaching down to take a pistol from the ground and firing it beneath the belly of his mount. He also trained one horse to sham death while he knelt beside it.

A number of others offered similar displays around this time. An increasing use of carriages had made learning equestrian skills less essential and therefore reduced the need for riding masters. They, and returning cavalrymen like Astley and Sampson, were looking for new employment. In cities such as London and Paris the decline of fairs, aggravated by the suppression of fairground-booth theatres, left acrobats and other entertainers looking for new performance opportunities.

Most, but not all, of the trick riders at this period worked their horses in a circle, partly perhaps because it is easier, though looking more dangerous, to stand on a horse that is galloping in a circle than on the straight, which means having to handle sharp corners. But a major consideration is that a ring offers the best chance for the largest number to see an act at close range. A crowd will spontaneously form a ring to watch any happening if there is nothing to prevent it.

Astley and his wife gave their first displays in June 1768. In July they added comedy to their show with a number based on a story which had already appeared in comic prints. It featured a London tailor who wanted to ride a few miles out of town to Brentford, in order to cast his vote for the radical John Wilkes, standing for election to Parliament. Philip Astley portrayed the tailor as Billy Button, an incompetent rider who at first cannot even mount his horse and when he does, cannot get it to move. Then it suddenly goes off at a gallop, throws him off its back and completes his humiliation by chasing him around the ring. This act was widely copied and joined the repertoire of performers in both Europe and America.

The earliest known occasion on which non-equestrian acts were added to a display of horsemanship occurred a few months later, in September 1768. At St George's Spaw, not far from Astley's pitch, a Mr Wilton and his lady partner, whom he had recently married, presented a rope dancer and tumbler between their own performances.

Astley had introduced clowning, Wilton acrobatics, and soon a variety of other acts were added to make a show that begins to be recognizable as what we call a circus. In 1769 Astley showed a 'learned' horse, did conjuring tricks as he galloped around on horseback, and introduced a duelling competition. Blackened sticks were used as swords and left visible marks on the contestants, who wore white outfits. Another innovation was a sack race with obstacles, the competitors wearing sacks over their heads which also enveloped their feet. By Christmas

Trained birds were another act seen in early circus performances, and one rider even had an act with bees. Wendy Salvador, showing her pigeons with the Austen Brothers Circus, is in the same tradition.

'Learned' horses remained a popular feature of circuses. This stock woodcut was used to promote them.

BELOW
Comic rides like that of the Tailor's Ride to Brentford became a staple of circus entertainment.

he had added tumbling to the bill. The following year, he had no competitors, and the 14-year old 'Master Griffiths' joined him as a rider. A covered stand was built to keep spectators dry when it rained. In July he announced that he was taking his little company to France, but he was back performing at Halfpenny Hatch for a week at Christmas. Next year he added new tricks, including one in which he picked up a coin from the ground while allegedly blindfolded and riding at full gallop. At the last performance of the season he introduced a trick in which he rode standing on two pint pots. Gradually, the equestrian repertoire expanded .

Early in the summer of 1771 another important personality, Charles Hughes, entered the picture. He must already have been an accomplished rider for he appears to have taken over at Halfpenny Hatch for a whole week in June before joining the Astley troop. He brought a comic act like Astley's tailor, involving a drunken sailor. He did not ride in the Christmas season. One account says he pleaded injury for leaving, but the following year, while Astley presented his little boy and another rider, he opened his own show, also on the south bank of the Thames, near Blackfriars Bridge.

Along with Hughes appeared his wife, her sister and a girl of eight years old in a programme much like that at Halfpenny Hatch. In another show he was billed as a 'puppet-show master', and probably manipulated marionettes as he rode around the ring in standing position. Later he was joined by another girl, 'the famous Miss Huntly, from Sadler's Wells,' a learner-rider called

TROUPE OF VERY REMARKABLE TRAINED PIGS.

PERFORMING NUMEROUS DIFFICULT, CLEVER & WONDERFUL TRICKS, ANIMALS SHOWING ALMOST HUMAN INTELLIGENCE & REASON. WHILE IN THE PERFORMANCE OF MANY CURIOUS & ORIGINAL FEATS

'Learned' pigs in 1898, more than a century after Astley's. One pig can chose cards and play a tune, the other two seem to have only one tune each, chosen to suit both American and Canadian or British audiences.

LEFT
When he had housed his circus in a covered building, Astley introduced a 'learned' pig. Such acts usually depend on movements or sounds, too small to be noticed by spectators, such as the clicking of a fingernail, to cue the animal to a particular response, choosing the right card or other token.

Jones, a tumbler, a conjurer, and a 'learned' horse. In his self-promotion Hughes claimed not only to have appeared before the King and Queen but also to have performed in Africa and America.

No supporting evidence has ever been produced to substantiate Hughes's claim to have appeared in America. The earliest recorded riding masters presenting public performances in the colonies were a Mr Faulks, who appeared in Philadelphia and New York in 1771 and also claimed to have performed before royalty in England, and an Englishman called John Sharp in Boston and Salem, Massachusetts, the same year. In 1772 another Englishman, Jacob Bates, was in America presenting his version of the Tailor's Ride to Brentford as well as other acts he had shown in Europe.

The rivalry between Astley and Hughes was acrimonious, and relations worsened further when Hughes not only employed Astley's father, whom Astley had thrown out after a quarrel, but even staged a benefit performance for him! However, competition compelled them, as well as other riding masters, to extend the range of their shows by introducing new kinds of performer. In 1773 Astley had a 'wise dog,' a furniture-balancing act (ingredients not specified), acrobats (including an Italian family who made a human pyramid), and a Spanish leaper and somersaulter. Hughes introduced trained birds, a violinist who played the instrument in unusual postures, and an Italian troupe who did conjuring on horseback. Another show, presented by a Mr Hyam at a pleasure garden in Brompton and for part of the week at Thomas Price's riding school in Islington, offered a slack-wire expert who balanced 13 full glasses on the end of a tobacco pipe, a family of Italian tightrope dancers, one of whom was also a leaper, and contortionists, as well as his own equestrian acts which included a version of the Tailor sketch.

In the following years Astley introduced a variety of other features, including fireworks and fountains, shadow puppets, a ventriloquist, a zebra, monkeys and a 'learned' pig'. Some acts took on a more dramatic form, with representations of the fall of the Bastille and of various military engagements.

Astley also improved facilities for his spectators. In 1769 he managed to find a patch of land to the south of Westminster Bridge, currently occupied unprofitably by a pheasantry, which he bought from its hard-up owner. Here he built a new ring, its performing area 60 feet (18 metres) across. The encircling spectators' area was roofed over and on one side a two- and three-storey structure provided wealthier patrons with more elegant accommodation, with stabling on either side below spectators' boxes. This main building was 51 feet (15 metres) high and was surmounted by a a a representation of a balancing equestrian advertising the entertainment to be seen within, while cloths hung on the outside walls which carried images of other feats, such as an 'Egyptian pyramid' of acrobats. Though performances were not affected by light rain, they could not continue in really bad weather and could only be given in daylight. Except for the Christmas holiday, they were restricted to the summer months, when they took place in the early evening. From 1772, Astley took his troupe to Paris in the autumn.

This arrangement continued for several years, but in the winter of 1778 Astley put on an evening entertainment in a room on Piccadilly while a new structure was erected at his riding-school site. It reopened in 1779 as Astley's Amphitheatre Riding House, and performances could now be given in all weathers and in the evening by artificial light. It is possible that the new 'Amphitheatre' coexisted for a time with the old riding ring, performances perhaps continuing in both. The building was apparently extended and improved in subsequent years, for by 1786 it had an interior painted with trees to give an outdoor effect and was called The

Royal Grove. One section of the seating was removed to make room for a small stage. There was more rebuilding in 1792, when the name became The Royal Saloon, but two years later, while Astley was in Europe with the British army, it was destroyed in a fire. It was rebuilt in 1795 as the Amphitheatre of Arts, then, after more rebuilding, as the Royal Amphitheatre in 1801. In 1803 Astley was again in France on military duties. He narrowly avoided imprisonment as an enemy alien, but escaped in disguise. When he reached London, he found his wife had died and his amphitheatre had again been destroyed by fire. Undaunted, he rebuilt it again on a grander scale.

That was not the last fire nor the last rebuilding, for the enterprise survived many years, long after the death of both Philip Astley and his son John, who had succeeded him. It always remained popularly known as Astley's, although bearing a variety of official names, under the last of which, George Sanger's National Amphitheatre, it was finally demolished in 1893.

At no time in any of its various incarnations was Astley's Amphitheatre ever officially given the name circus. It was Charles Hughes, and the partners with whom he set it up, who were first to use that name – for the 'Royal Circus' which they opened in 1782. The idea came from Charles Dibdin, a composer and dramatist who had formerly held a house post at the Theatre Royal in Covent Garden. He thought he could present riding displays much more elegantly than the riding masters, combining equestrianism with drama. He raised money from backers, one of whom provided the site, and himself became both manager and dramatist. Hughes supplied the equestrian contribution, and Giuseppe Grimaldi, ballet master at the Theatre Royal, Drury Lane, was engaged to train a chorus of twenty children. The premises comprised an attractive theatre with neoclassical auditorium and a small stage from which the action could descend into the central ring.

The Royal Circus and Equestrian Philharmonic Academy opened in November 1782 with a pantomime ballet, but the proprietors failed to obtain the necessary licence and after nine performances, just as they looked like having a successful Christmas season, they were forced to close. By the time the licence was obtained, Dibdin was hiding from creditors. Grimaldi briefly replaced him, and a summer season was mounted in competition with Astley's. There were difficulties with the backers and, when Dibdin did return, he quarrelled with Hughes and they parted company. Attempts to combine horses and legitimate drama foundered, as the licence did not permit straight plays to be presented. When a clown called Carlo Delpini staged some elaborate mixed-media productions a number of the actors were arrested for delivering dialogue.

Shows had to be a mixture of pantomime, ballet and spectacle, and included fireworks (the stage roof could be opened to let out the smoke). Although Hughes was official manager in 1784-89, from the time Grimaldi departed until Delpini took over, and although he was in continual conflict with the proprietors, he did have some

Astley's Riding School near Westminster Bridge in 1777, engraved after a drawing by William Capon. The central posts are typical of riding schools where actual instruction was given. The central figure in the 60-foot (18 metres) ring appears to be a clown.

The Royal Circus, built for Charles Hughes, was in competition with Astley's. Ramps allow action to be carried down into the ring. Equestrian dramas and musical entertainments were presented as well as circus.

successes. One of his grand finales in 1785 featured a hunt at Windsor with horses and twelve pairs of hounds chasing a fox. Its success led to an even more ambitious stag hunt. There were acrobats and tightrope walkers, pantomimes and historical spectacles. In 1791 elaborate scenery was painted for a presentation of the Fall of the Bastille, and in the same year the Royal Circus engaged one of Astley's best clowns, whose name was Porter. Another artist was Peter Ducrow, known as the 'Flemish Hercules', who could leap over seven horses and through a circle of fire 14 feet in the air. Patrons could see all the kinds of act that were presented at Astley's Amphitheatre, which acknowledged the quality of its rival by copying the Royal Circus spectacles. However, Astley was probably the greater showman and, as owner of his enterprise, he was not hindered by the problems with proprietors which beset Hughes.

By 1793 Hughes had had enough and decided to go abroad. When he returned he arranged to lease the Royal Circus to others. He died not long afterwards and, after a brief period of success the Royal Circus was burned down. Rebuilt, it did only poor business until, with the ring removed, it became popular as the Surrey Theatre, a simple playhouse which occasionally reverted to presenting circus entertainments.

With Astley and Hughes almost all the elements of modern circus, including the name, had been brought together, from rope dancers, clowns, equestrians and trained animals to the grand spectacle that became such a feature of American circus in its heyday. According to a description in Decastro's memoirs, one spectacle in 1791 included leopards and tigers drawing carts around the ring, but these may have been men in skins rather than real animals. Wild-animal shows, apart from dancing bears and monkeys, were confined to the menageries, such as the one exhibited in London at the Exeter Exchange in the Strand, or the menagerie of Mr Pidock which toured Britain in the 1780s. The menagerie was later to become an important partner of the circus, but the appearance of the first lion tamers in the ring was still far off.

The Spread of the Circus

Several of the riding masters claimed to have performed internationally and both Philip Astley and Charles Hughes appeared on the Continent. Astley gave regular seasons in Paris from 1772 until the outbreak of war in 1778. When hostilities ceased in 1783 Queen Marie Antoinette sent for the whole company. Performing at Versailles, the young John Astley was a particular success and the Queen gave him a gold medal set with diamonds. In Paris Astley gave his performances in the open air at the Faubourg du Temple, and such was his success that he decided to build a permanent indoor amphitheatre on the site in 1783. In France, as in

Astley's Amphitheatre in the early 19th century, depicted by Pugin and Thomas Rowlandson. This was the final form that Astley himself knew, though it was rebuilt again in 1841.

England, the theatres were protected from unlicensed competition and in 1787 Astley was informed that, although his riding displays were acceptable, the tumbling acts that he was showing infringed the law. He circumvented this difficulty rather ingeniously. He had a large wooden platform constructed, which was supported on the backs of a number of horses, technically converting the offending tumbling act into an equestrian display.

The French Revolution temporarily ended Astley's appearances in Paris and from 1791 to 1802 the Amphitheatre was taken over by Antonio Franconi, a Venetian who had originally been a menagerie cage boy

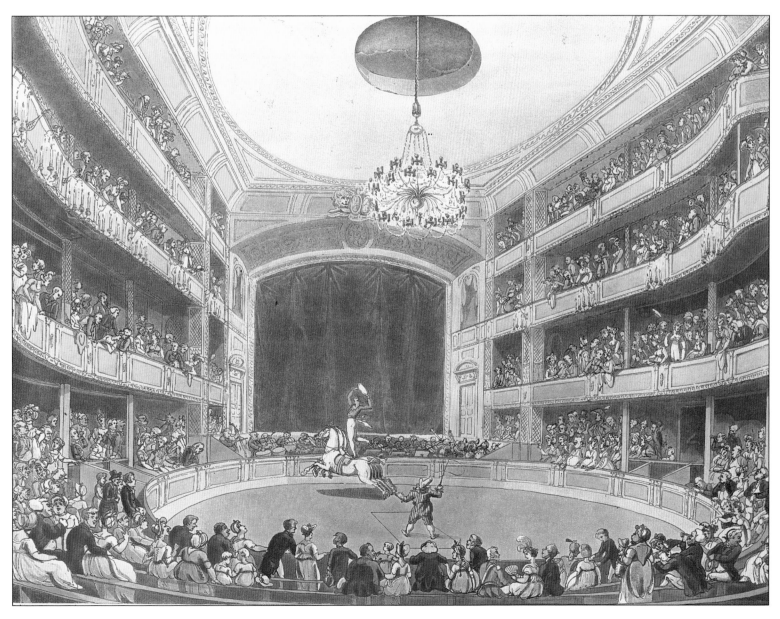

and fled to France after fighting a duel. He appeared at the Amphitheatre in 1783 with a bird act and later became an equestrian. In 1786 he started his own circus. When Astley returned to Paris in 1802 Franconi, whose family remained prominent in circus history throughout the 19th century, moved his riding shows to the Eclos des Capucins and in 1807 to the Cirque Olympique, returning to the Amphitheatre (which he renamed also Cirque Olympique) ten years later. Franconi's family, sometimes in collaboration with Louis Dejean, ran another Olympique from 1827 and when that was turned into a conventional theatre, they were at the Cirque d'Eté and the Cirque d'Hiver, still the primary home of circus in Paris.

Astley is said to have built 19 circuses in Britain and Europe. He was active beyond France. He was certainly in Brussels for a time and may have reached Vienna and even Belgrade. Both he and his son John died in Paris.

Charles Hughes was responsible for taking the circus to Russia. About 1790, withdrawing from the problems and quarrels at the Royal Circus, he accepted an invitation to buy good English stallions and mares to be sent to Russia to improve breeding stock. He agreed to accompany his purchases to St Petersburg, and also took his Royal Circus horses with him. His performances in the Russian capital proved popular with the Empress Catherine and the court. Decastro implies, in his account, that Hughes became one of Catherine's many lovers (she was then over 60), but by 1793 he was back in England. Although it would be another eight decades before a native Russian circus company was formed in St Petersburg, Hughes had laid the foundations of a great circus tradition. It was the culmination of his own career, for he died in 1797.

James Price, perhaps a son of Thomas Price of the Islington Riding School, travelled to Austria, Constantinople, Germany and Denmark before, with a company of rope dancers and trick riders, he followed Hughes to St Petersburg in 1795 and settled there. The name Price also appears as that of a lady rider in the circus of Christoph de Bach which had a permanent base in Vienna, at the Circus Gymnasticus in the Prater, Vienna, and toured other European capitals. She married the Italian Alessandro Guerra, known as Il Furioso, who developed a circus in Italy which also toured Russia.

As the 19th century progressed there were many others – riding masters, rope dancers and acrobats – who formed circuses across Europe. Among those of lasting importance was the circus founded by Friedrich Knie, son of an Innsbruck doctor not of showman stock, who ran away to join a circus and then set up his own company. At the time of the Franco-Prussian War (1880) it was established in Switzerland and, now known as the Swiss National Circus (though still a private company), it remains there today .

Equally famous was the Circus Renz founded by Ernst Jacob Renz. Born in 1815, son of a rope dancer, he was apprenticed to a horse trainer called Rudolph Brilloff and by the age of 14 had also acquired the skills of a good all-round acrobat and clown. He started his own Cirque Equestre in the Karlstrasse in Berlin and others in Hamburg, Breslau and Vienna. One of his riders was Gotthold Schumann, who left to set up his own circus in 1870. His family have been famous as equestrians and horse trainers ever since. One son, Albert, founded circuses in Vienna and Frankfurt, and took over the Renz circus in Berlin. Another son, Max, set up a circus in Copenhagen and in effect founded Scandinavian circus.

In Britain permanent circus buildings were erected in several cities besides London before the end of the 18th century, in addition to temporary structures used by touring circuses. While his father was in Paris, Philip Astley's son John took on much of the responsibility not only for running the Amphitheatre and touring companies

A handbill for Philip and John Astley's performances in Paris in 1786, as Jacob Decastro reproduced it in his memoirs, 1824. Their tumbling was not allowed so, by placing their stage on horseback, they made it an entirely equestrian show.

RIGHT
Bill for Batty's Circus Royal in Leamington, a temporary structure. Hengler (who presented himself as French) had been at the Royal Circus in 1803. The boy and his two brothers erected permanent buildings in several cities including their Circus in London.

but also for confronting stiff competition from a consortium of five leading performers. With the 1804 rebuilding of the Amphitheatre they joined forces, the consortium taking a half share.

Other circuses were soon touring Britain and a number of performers appeared who achieved lasting fame either as individuals or as the founders of circus dynasties. Among them was the strongman and leaper Peter Ducrow, the 'Flemish Hercules', whose son Andrew became the most famous, though not necessarily the best, of all riders. There was the equestrian Jack Clarke, who appeared at the Royal Circus and in the provinces for several years before starting his own circus. He trained his daughter as a child equestrian; later generations excelled as riders and a grandson created a flying trapeze act. There was Thomas Taplin Cooke who formed a daily circus, took it to America and overcame a series of disasters, starting again from scratch. His descendants were to be found throughout the circus world, among their acts the Clarkonians, a group of acrobats with 69 members. The sons of a rope dancer at the Royal Circus called Hengler created their own circus and made their name famous. The façade of their grand circus in Argyll Street, London, converted from the Corinthian Bazaar in 1871, still survives, although the interior was rebuilt as the now equally famous theatre, the London Palladium. It survived longer than any other permanent circus building in Britain and was famous for a ring that could be flooded, like that at the Nouveau Cirque in Paris built in 1886. Such a device, permitting aquatic spectaculars, was

W. Cocking. Del.

MR DUCROW AS MERCURY.

Pub. by M.&M. SKELT, 11. Swan St Minories. London.

R. Lloyd. Sculp
Plate 5.

entertainments as they did of stage plays and even music making, but nevertheless professional entertainers were to be found even in New England. In 1724 one troupe announced in the *Weekly Mercury* that it would be appearing in Philadelphia at the New Booth, that city's first theatre on Society Hill, in the 'famous Performance of Roap-dancing, which is to be performed to the Admiration of all the Beholders'. It was to be given:

'1st, By a little Boy of seven Years old, who Dances and Capers upon the strait Roap, to the Wonder of all Spectators.
2dly, By a Woman, who Dances a Corant and a Jigg upon the Roap, which she performs as well as any Dancing Master does it on the Ground.
3dly, She Dances with Baskets upon her Feet, and iron Fetters upon her Legs.
4thly, She walks upon the Roap with a Wheel-Barrow before her.
5thly, You will see various Performances upon the Slack Roap.
6thly, You are entertained with the Comical Humour of your Old Friend Pickle Herring.
The whole Concluded with a Woman turning round in a swift Motion with seven or eight Swords Points at her Eyes, Mouth and Breast, for a Quarter of an Hour together, to the Admiration of all that behold the Performance.

There will likewise be several other diverting Performances on the Stage, too large here to mention.'
Performances were to be at seven in the evening

later copied at Astley's, the London Hippodrome, at the Tower in Blackpool and the Hippodrome in Great Yarmouth.

The biggest circus name in Britain in the later 19th century was 'Lord' George Sanger. His ex-sailor father toured fairs with a roundabout and a peepshow and George and his brother John tried a magic-lantern booth, conjuring, and an act with trained birds and mice before launching a small circus show in 1853. They had no circus skills themselves but got themselves a 'learned' pony and a ring-trained horse, hired three experienced performers and roped in the younger members of their family as assistants. In the first year they added a score of horses and after three years had a stable of 60 horses, plus a group of six lions. After nearly 20 years of increasing success they separated, John leaving to organize his own circus. In 1871 George bought Astley's, which he ran until it was demolished in 1893 to make way for the building of St Thomas's Hospital. He ran the country's largest touring circus, had circus buildings in several cities and a winter circus in London's Agricultural Hall.

Although 'Lord' George Sanger did present his circus before an enthusiastic Queen Victoria, his title was bestowed by himself. He thought it would add a touch of class to the name of his circus. The knighthood implied by the Sir Robert Fossett Circus is also a masquerade.

The circus had its origin in a bird act and toured Britain right up to 1992. Its acts still tour around Europe and have plans to reform in Britain when economic conditions permit. Another circus with humble beginnings as a bird act was begun by Jean-Pierre Ginette, a French soldier captured at the Battle of Waterloo who decided to make his life in England and worked with four canaries.

He too bought a pony, trained it to tell fortunes and established a family equestrian act. Eventually he owned a touring circus and circus buildings and became the ancestor of two circus families. The circus was taken to America almost as soon as it had been established in Europe. Of course, acrobats and other separate acts, sometimes combining humour with balancing feats, already existed in the American colonies. The Puritan New England settlements disapproved of such

TOP
The sumptuous Cirque des Champs-Elysées, Paris, in 1843. Circus became very fashionable in France. Here, while the balletic equestrian jumps through a hoop and prepares to leap over ribbons, a foreground clown has fallen from his stool.

ABOVE
An advertisement for Astley's Amphitheatre in 1843. William Batty ran an equestrian company from the 1820s, put his circus under canvas in 1843, and while Astley's was being rebuilt, ran the Olympic Circus in London and in 1851-53 his Hippodrome in Kensington near the 1851 Exhibition at the Crystal Palace.

for 20 days and prices were quite high: one shilling and sixpence in the gallery, two shillings in the pit and three shillings for seats on the stage. This was typical of the kind of show to be seen in booths or in the open air at European fairs, with a clown – Pickle Herring – as well as acrobats.

Exotic animals were occasionally exhibited at this time, but singly and shown as curiosities, not performers. According to published records there was a lion in Boston in 1720. Possibly it was the same animal shown a few years later in Philadelphia and New York, for it is always referred to as The Lyon, and the next mention of a lion in the public press does not occur until 1791. A camel was advertised for viewing in Boston in 1721, and a polar bear in 1733. Another camel (or perhaps the same one) was in Philadelphia and New York in 1739-40 and a pair were reported in 1787. The first elephant to be seen in America arrived in 1796. In 1781 a collection of birds, reptiles, snakes and quadrupeds was being shown in New York, though it is not clear from the announcement whether

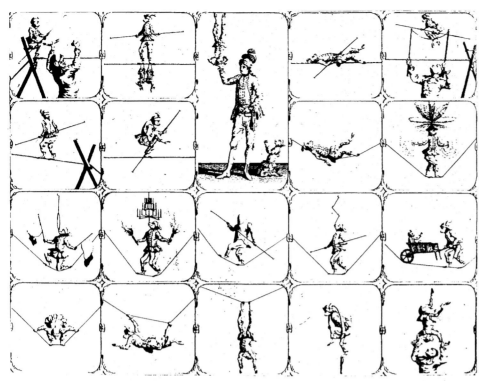

these were live or stuffed animals, and in 1789 a New York exhibition included a crocodile, orang-utan, baboon, tame tiger (perhaps a jaguar or other cat), ant bear, lizard, snakes, porcupine, swordfish and a variety of birds. By that time the first travelling menageries were beginning to tour in the newly independent United States, and some smaller animals were taught tricks. A performing monkey is reported in 1751 and though no more are recorded until 1788, performing dogs and trained birds were no doubt familiar; a 'learned' pig is reported at Boston in 1798.

British trick riders began to appear in the 1770s. Charles Hughes claimed to have been in America in 1771 but John Sharp is the first on record. He performed at Boston in that year, riding standing on two horses with a third between. A man named Faulks, who claimed to have appeared before British royalty, appeared in Philadelphia and New York the same year. His repertoire included playing a French horn while standing on horseback and vaulting between three horses. The next year Jacob Bates was in Philadelphia and in 1773 New York, at the Bulls Head in the Bowery, presenting his version of 'The Tailor's Ride to Brentford'.

Dissatisfaction in the colonies was now reaching a head, soon to become armed revolution in the War of Independence. In that atmosphere, society did not smile on such frivolous activities as circus. In 1774 the colonial representatives meeting in Philadelphia in the first Continental Congress formally forbade such shows and exhibitions.

When independence had been achieved and the new nation began to settle down, riding displays reappeared. A man named Pool was active in Baltimore, Boston and Philadelphia in 1785, in New York the following year, and he later travelled south to Georgia. He billed his humorous Tailor as riding to New York rather than Brentford, and announced himself as 'the first American' to give such exhibitions. Actually, he had been described as English in the West Indies a few years earlier, so he was probably not American-born. That does not of course negate his claim, which gives him a small place in circus history. However, it was a newcomer from England who raised the circular building at the corner of 12th and Market Streets in Philadelphia in 1792 that is generally considered the first real circus in the United States. He was the rider John Bill Ricketts, trained by Charles Hughes and already successful in London and Edinburgh before he crossed the Atlantic. The original building, a simple, fenced arena, was a temporary

Signor Spinacuta and his trained monkey. The engraving was made when he performed at Sadler's Wells, London. He then went to America with Ricketts and became one of America's circus pioneers.

structure, and was replaced two years later by the Pantheon or Amphitheatre in Chestnut Street. The site of the original structure is now marked by a circular piazza and a plaque.

'The programme for 22 April 1793, when George Washington attended a performance, described Ricketts's display, somewhat confusingly though at great length:

Mr Ricketts leaps over a riband suspended twelve feet high and at the same time through a cane held in both hands and alights on the other side with his feet on the saddle, the horse being in full speed; he hangs by one leg, sweeps both hands and the plume of his cap on the ground, likewise mounts his horse in full speed, with one foot on the saddle in a pleasing attitude; he rides a single horse, turning round like the fly of a Jack, vaulting from the horse to the ground and from thence to the horse, likewise from the near side to the off side, and from thence to the near side; he stands on the saddle and puts himself in various graceful attitudes, the horse in full gallop; he will ride a single horse, standing erect, and throw up a bottle and marble, playing with the same in the air, then receives the marble in the mouth of the bottle, the horse being in full gallop; he throws up an orange and receives it on the point of a sword, at the same time standing on the saddle without the assistance of bridle reins, turns about and throws a somerset; he will ride two horses standing erect at the same time throwing up two oranges and a fork, playing with them in the air, and receives the orange on the point of the fork; he will put a glass of wine in a hoop, turning it round rapidly, the glass remaining at the same time in its place, takes the same and drinks to the company, the horse being in full gallop, and all without the assistance of the reins; he rides a single horse in full gallop, standing on his head on the saddle at the same time; he will perform a hornpipe on a single horse, with and without the bridle, likewise leaps from his horse to the ground and with the same spring leaps from the ground with one foot on the saddle in the attitude of Mercury, the horse being in full gallop; he rides a single horse, springs from the seat erect without touching the saddle with his hands, then forms the attitude of Mercury without the assistance of the reins; he leaps from the horse to the ground and with the same spring remounts with his face towards the horse's tail and throws a somerset backward; the whole to conclude with Mr. Ricketts carrying his young pupil on his shoulders in the attitude of Mercury, standing on two horses in full gallop.'

Ricketts's brought his brother Francis with him to America but he seems to have recruited the rest of his company after his arrival. They included Signor Spinacuta, a French (despite the name) rope dancer, clown, tumbler and animal trainer; a clown called McDonald, and a horse called Cornplanter. Bought in New York, Cornplanter would find and pick up a hidden handkerchief and could remove its own saddle. Ricketts was keen to hire a wire walker called John Durang, and two years later succeeded. By that time his company had grown to 17, including Mr Sully from Charleston, Mr Franklin who had been a rider and clown at London's Royal Circus, and a group of Native American chiefs, plus a band, carpenters and painters. He built two circuses in New York, in Greenwich Street and at the bottom of Broadway, and included pantomime sketches in the bill. In 1793, after Washington had paid another visit to the circus, Ricketts arranged to buy the President's 27-year-old horse, not as a performer but simply to exhibit it as 'the celebrated horse Jack, who was in the American War with General Washington, and [was] presented to Mr Ricketts', a clever way of implying the President's endorsement of his show. The brothers split the company into two much smaller circuses. John, with a troupe including Durang and two others, went to Canada. They played a week at Albany on the way and had such success at Montreal that he built a stone circus for the winter. It

POSITIVELY THE LAST NIGHT of Mr. VILALLIAVE's Company, at HATHAWAY's HALL, on MONDAY evening next, the 17th of August, 1818.

THE PERFORMANCE WILL COMMENCE BY THE

TIGHT ROPE,

WITH BALANCE POLE.

1st Performer.	The *Little Chinese.*
2d.	The *Young Spaniolet.*
3d.	The *Young Roman.*
4th.	Mrs. *Vilalliave.*
5th.	Mr. *Vilalliave.*
6th.	Mr. *Begodes*, in the character of a CLOWN.

Among the great variety of Feats which they will perform, Mr. VILALLIAVE will dance on the Rope

A GROTESQUE DANCE,

With a BASKET tied to his Feet, and his Hands and Feet chained.

THERE WILL LIKEWISE BE EXHIBITED,

The Dance of the Double Rope,

BY THREE PERSONS, *(as represented in the Plate above.)*

They will afterwards perform a great variety without the Balance Pole, too numerous to be inserted.

BENDING FEATS,

BY THE CHINESE AND YOUNG SPANIOLET.

TUMBLING,

BY THE COMPANY.

Strength of Hercules,

OR,

The Egyptian Pyramid;

Performed by Mr. VILALLIAVE.

The Publick are respectfully informed, that there will be no pains or exertion spared, to give a brilliant Exhibition.

** Doors open at half past 7, and the Performance to commence at 8 o'clock, precisely.

August 15, 1818.

An advertisement for Mr Vilalliave's company in 1818.

incorporated a full stage with doors on to the apron, a curtain and scenery. After another two months in Quebec they returned well content to Philadelphia. Francis, on the other hand, had a disastrous tour and had to sell his horses.

After John got back to Philadelphia, a carelessly left candle in the carpenter's workshop set fire to the building during a performance. It was completely destroyed, though they managed to save the horses, scenery and costumes. John took the circus south and on his return to Philadelphia negotiated to perform in a circus built by a rival French troupe, which had arrived in America in 1796. The French, led by Philip Lailson, had

been joined by at least two American riders, a Mr Langley and a Miss Venice, and performed in Boston and at Greenwich Street in New York before President John Adams, as well as in Philadelphia, but they too met with disaster when the dome of their elegant circus collapsed under the weight of winter snow. At the time the company had left to try their luck in the West Indies. In 1801 Ricketts decided to do the same but the ship on which he sailed was captured by pirates. He managed to extricate himself and his horses and performed successfully in the Leeward Islands but, after the death of two of his company and the jailing of his brother for deserting his native-born wife, only one performer besides himself was left, so he sold his horses and took ship again for England. His luck failed to improve. The vessel was lost at sea and there were no survivors.

A year after Ricketts's first appearance in New York, Thomas Swan was there exhibiting his horsemanship in what was now clearly described as the Circus: it may have been Ricketts's Broadway Amphitheatre. He featured a local-born equestrienne, Miss Johnson, and a rope-dancing monkey, the first evidence of an animal act in America other than horses.

The new century saw other arrivals from Europe. In 1807 the mainly French company of Pepin and Breschard (though Pepin had been born in Albany, New York, of French parents) was successful in New York and erected its own circus in Philadelphia before splitting into two smaller troupes in 1810. One, led by Cayetano with Codet, Menial and Redons, featured a performing elephant in New York in 1812 and advertised Mrs Redon as the first American lady circus rider. The others toured first as Dwyer and Breschard's Circus, then as Twait and Breschard, before they all rejoined forces in 1813 as Pepin, Breschard and Cayetano.

The following year Mr Vilalliave advertised his New York Circus, though it really consisted of rope acts and acrobats and performed in halls rather than the ring. They also sang songs and enacted a pantomime. An 1818 bill announces items by Vilalliave, his wife, their clown Begodes, a 'little Chinese,' a 'young Roman' and a 'young Spaniolet,' though whether these names reflected their nationalities or the nature of their acts is not clear. A 'Dance of the Double Rope' featured two people on the tightrope with a third balancing on what appears to have been a bar with terminal yokes placed around their shoulders, rather than a rope.

In 1816 James West, formerly of Astley's and the Royal Circus in London, arrived with a company which included a rider and rope dancer called Blackmore who, in London three years later, was given star status at Astley's as 'the young American', though West may have brought him over from England to America in the first place. After six successful years in America, West sold his show to two theatre managers and it became Price and Simpson's Broadway Circus. West went back to England a rich man and became a partner of Andrew Ducrow at Astley's. In his last New York season his clown, Williams, who was also a leaper, jumped over a wagon and six horses, and over a camel and an elephant – animals presumably acquired in America. The new proprietors engaged another Astley's acrobatic rider and rope dancer, Mr Hunter (later known as the 'Yorkshire Phenomenon'), who rode bareback (others used either a saddle or a pad which made it easier to balance). European performers continued to cross the Atlantic, but the movement was now in both directions, with American acts billed with circuses in Europe.

In New York, Charles Sandford erected a circus building in 1825, the Lafayette Amphitheatre, among property he was developing in the Canal Street area, but the following year it was converted into an orthodox theatre, whereupon Sandford built the Mount Pitt Circus in Broome Street. Seating 3,500 people, it was said to be the biggest place of entertainment in America, but it was

WALNUT STREET THEATRE

NINTH AND WALNUT STS., PHILADELPHIA.

SOLE LESSEE, - - - - MRS. M. A. GARRETTSON
STAGE MANAGER, - - - - MR. G. VINING BOWERS
BUSINESS AGENT, - - - - MR. J. T. DONNELLY

Doors open at quarter to 7. The Curtain will rise at quarter past 7

Re-Engagement, and Positively Last Night but Three of

DAN RICE

THE GREATEST LIVING HUMORIST,

Together with his MODEL TROUPE of EQUESTRIANS.

WEDNESDAY, MARCH 12th, 1862

Come Boys and have some Fun.

A Ride on Dan Rice's Mules.

TWO Performances

THIS DAY!

In the AFTERNOON, ESPECIALLY for FAMILY PARTIES, commencing at half past 2 o'clk.

Great Success of MADAM TOURNAIRE

And her Wonderful Horse, KOLB.

Madam Tournaire in Two Acts.

A bill for Dan Rice's circus in Philadelphia, 1862. He invites spectators to try to ride his mules, a feature of many circuses. A horse would sometimes be trained to act like a bucking bronco until a little girl was placed on the saddle, when it would behave perfectly.

LEFT
Dan Rice.

destroyed by a fire in 1829. James W. Bancker started his New York Circus in 1826, apparently the first set up by an American proprietor, and many others appeared about this time. There were 17 advertised in 1828 and in the 1830s over 30 were on the road in various parts of the United States.

Touring proved essential to success: attempts at permanent circuses did not succeed. Hitherto, travelling circuses had performed in temporary timber structures, but now they began to use tents. The first circus to use a tent set it up in a New York pleasure garden in 1823, and within a few years tents were adopted by touring circuses. As a tent could be put up and lowered much more quickly, it became practicable to perform in smaller towns that warranted only a brief stay. Tents were also much easier to transport than the timber required to build an arena.

There was still some prejudice against such entertainments, and the circus was by no means welcome everywhere in the United States. In 1798 Connecticut had strengthened its anti-circus law and the rider Hunter was prosecuted under it in 1826. He afterwards returned to England, where he appeared for the next decade until he ran into trouble in Liverpool in 1839. He upset some of his fellow artistes sufficiently for an American horseman, Ben Stickley, to report him to the police for stealing a coat, which he had apparently picked up accidentally. Stickley's intention was probably just to give him a fright, but once started the legal process was unstoppable and the unfortunate Hunter was sentenced to transportation to Australia!

American tours began to extend farther westward. One circus reached Chillicothe, Ohio, in 1813, only to be attacked by the local newspaper: 'Believing that these men are prosecuting an unlawful calling – one that cannot be defended on Scriptural ground or on the principles of sound reason and good policy, we presume that the good sense of the citizens in general would lead them to treat their exhibitions with that unqualified neglect and contempt which they so justly deserve.'

Menageries, which could be considered educational rather than entertaining, were more acceptable than circuses, though by the1820s they had also begun to feature elephants and monkeys performing tricks. They seem to have travelled farther than the the circuses, although large and dangerous animals were not easy to transport in their cages. Menageries began to make use of canvas walls to screen their exhibits from those who had not paid admission, and they used large tents before they were taken up by circuses.

Before the 19th century few roads were suitable for wheeled vehicles. In Britain it was only with the work of engineers such as John McAdam and Thomas Telford, and the creation of the turnpike trusts, that long-distance roads began to be laid which did not turn into a quagmire in wet weather. Otherwise, conditions were bad in Europe and even worse in America. West of the Appalachians, roads were little more than trails, making it difficult for a touring troupe to carry more than basic equipment.

Wherever possible it was much easier to travel by water. The Great Lakes and the Ohio and Mississippi systems gave access to many communities, and the opening of the Erie Canal in 1825 made access easier between New York and the Midwest. At first, ordinary boats were used to carry the circus, which disembarked and set up its tents at each location. The equestrian and clown Dan Rice transported his circus in this way on the Allegheny Mail in 1848, but by mid-century river boats were built which incorporated the circus ring and arena.

The *Floating Palace*, built at Cincinnati for the Spalding and Rogers Circus in 1851 at a cost of $42,000 and inaugurated at Pittsburg in 1852, consisted of a large barge which was pushed in front of a stern-wheel paddleboat. It contained a full-size circus ring, 42 feet (12.6 metres) in diameter, and could accommodate 3,400 spectators. All this fitted on a barge 250 feet (75 metres) long and 60 feet (18 metres) wide. It was lit by gas and heated by hot water from steam boilers. After the invention of the calliope, or steam organ, in 1856, one was installed on the *Floating Palace*. Its harsh and extremely loud whistling notes announced the coming of the circus far in advance of its arrival.

The *Floating Palace* plied the Ohio and Mississippi rivers until the coming of the Civil War. In 1854 Spalding and Rogers leased the Amburgh and Raymond Menagerie and exhibited it on board, and in 1855 they introduced 'curiosities' and stage shows on the steamer. After the outbreak of the Civil War, the boat was tied up at New Albany in Indiana while the circus travelled to South America. After the war, fire destroyed the *Floating Palace* so it was never used again.

In 1857 the enterprising Spalding and Rogers made an attempt at touring by railroad, but it was not successful. Another decade was to pass before this new form of transport began to attract much circus custom.

Some US circuses travelled far afield. Equestrian Joseph A. Rowe, for instance, took his circus to Peru in the 1840s. He was there when he heard about the Gold Rush in California in 1849, and promptly took ship for San Francisco. Only 17 days after his arrival the West Coast had its first circus, housed in a theatre on Kearney Street. Rowe stayed there a year, then went off to Australia and the South Seas. He made a fortune and retired in 1854, but was tempted back to California two years later. Sadly for him, the boom was over. He kept going, touring California in 1857, then tried another season in Australia but failed to reproduce his earlier profits. He had to close the show and work for other circuses.

Circus and menagerie were drawing closer together. Sometimes the same site would be used by a circus in the afternoon and a menagerie in the evening. In 1817 the Theatre of Natural Curiosity at Warren Street in New York had shown camels and various other animals along with a group of gymnasts and rope dancers, but the first to tour both together appears to have been A. J. Purdy in 1832 (his circus may also have been the first to tour in a tent). An 1837 poster for the tour of the menagerie of the Bowery-based Zoological Institute makes it clear that there was a ring attached, and they employed a clown called Daniel Drew. One of their animal keepers was Isaac Van Amburgh, soon to become the most famous of the early lion tamers, though by no means the first, and he was already boldly entering the

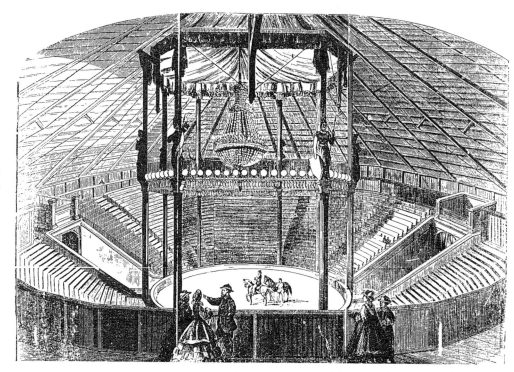

The Hippotheatron, on Broadway and 14th Street in New York, opened in 1864 under James Cooke's management and was run by Lewis Lent, so that it became known as Lent's Iron Building. America's only permanent, intimate, circus building, it was taken over by Phineas Barnum in 1872 but, though built of iron, it burned down later that year.

big-cat cages as one of the spectacles offered to the public. In 1838 they converted their New York menagerie into a a central-ring circus under the name the Bowery Amphitheatre and in following decades many of the leading circuses appeared there.

The Institute had been formed in 1835 by a group of 135 young farmers from the Somers area of New York State who had been speculating in menageries and circuses. The complete group lasted for only a couple of years but four of them – John J. June, Lewis B. Titus, Cabel Sutton Angevine and Jeremiah Crane, all from North Salem – remained. They called themselves the 'Syndicate' and later earned the name of the 'Flatfoots' from the way they declared that they 'put their foot down flat' in claiming some areas as their exclusive territory. The 'Flatfoots' remained a powerful force for the next half century, buying up circuses or forming partnerships to maintain their control.

The history of American circus is one of fierce competition with frequent takeovers, partnerships and separations, names being confusingly revived or appropriated. Touring shows posted their own bills over those of their competitors, put up notices on the lines of 'don't waste your dollars, wait for the real show!', and attempted to find out rivals' scheduled touring dates in order to appear ahead of them.

The scale of shows varied enormously. One of the early tenting circuses, Quick and Mead, is said to have had a tent only 50 feet (15 metres) across. The whole show, except the ring curb that separated performers from audience, could be carried on a two-horse wagon. Buckley and Weeks, with a tent half as big again that could house an audience of 800, toured with a company of 35 and 40 horses, requiring eight wagons. It was not long before much bigger companies took to the road or, increasingly, the railroad. As the century progressed American circus came to be dominated by a handful of large circuses presenting performances in a style that was uniquely American.

The Floating Palace, *Spalding and Rogers' circus barge.*

MARKS'S NEW PORTRAIT.

*American lion tamer Isaac Van
Amburgh, a success on both sides of
the Atlantic, depicted at the time he
was appearing at Astley's in London
in 1838.*

The Golden Age of the Circus

During the latter part of the 19th century, especially in America, some circuses developed into massive operations putting on ever more spectacular shows. Competition between circuses and between artists encouraged constant innovation in developing new acts and new levels of daring acrobatic achievement. The wealth of talent and the enthusiasm of audiences, from the first continental tours through to the 1930s, combined to create a golden age of circus, an age characterized by outrageous hype and tremendous panache, in which the circus brought colour and spectacle to places that saw little of either before the days of cinema and television. The best part of a century later, acrobats are still performing ever more amazing feats and spectacles are staged that would have boggled the minds of our ancestors, but nostalgia for the old days, nourished by stories of past performers and the impact of old posters and publicity, suggests a world full of drama and romance that we have lost. Of course, it was not entirely like that.

A few big names recur in the history of American circus: Robinson, Bailey, Sells, Forepaugh and of course Barnum and Ringling. The story is confused by names like Robinson and Bailey that were shared by several proprietors and by the fact that names became a trading perquisite taken over by other companies.

Hachaliah Bailey, for instance, was a menagerie owner who was exhibiting an elephant called Bet in 1809. He never ran a circus, though at one time he was an associate of Nathan ('Uncle Nat') Howes who, some say, was the first American to put together and tour a regular circus troupe. James Augustus ('Gus') Bailey started a circus with Molly Kirkland just before the Civil War and ran one for many years afterwards (he also wrote the song 'The Old Grey Mare'), but James Bailey was actually born McGinnis and took his name from Frederick Harrison Bailey, a very distant relation of Hachaliah who was advance man with the Robinson and Lake Circus and got him a job, later adopting him as a son. James Bailey became an astute circus manager, buying interests in other circuses and eventually going into partnership with P. T. Barnum. Another Bailey, George Fox Bailey, was a nephew of Hachaliah who talked his father-in-law Aaron Turner into leasing animals from the Syndicate to run a combined circus-menagerie, a pattern soon followed by other Syndicate shows. George Fox Bailey later inherited Aaron's circus and toured under various names until 1875. Before he died, in 1904, he was calling himself 'the last of the Flatfoots'.

John Robinson, performer as well as proprietor, is alleged to have started his circus in 1824, when he was 22. He toured first as Robinson and Foster, becoming very popular in the South. He too had an adopted son, James Michael Fitzgerald, who took the Robinson name and became a master equestrian, popularizing bareback riding in America. Sometimes in partnership, and under various names, the Robinson family circus continued on the road until 1938.

A bareback equestrienne performing in Denver, Colorado, probably in the 1920s. Bareback riding was not introduced until 1820 and not widely seen until later. The tutu-like skirt was a mid-19th century development but the atmosphere must be like that of the earliest tented circuses.

ABOVE RIGHT
The larger circuses had their own railroad rolling stock. They used the railroad to transport the circus but also hired special excursion trains to bring in spectators from all around, increasing the catchment area for a single stand, as shown in this poster of 1896.

Fayette Lodawick ('Yankee') Robinson had been an actor in Shakespeare before he became a clown, a lion trainer, and finally proprietor of his own circus in 1854. It was popular touring the Midwest and northeast after the Civil War until 1876, when its proprietor reverted to his former calling with a touring repertory theatre. He was often at pains to disassociate his show from that of John Robinson. In 1883 the Ringling Brothers invited him to join them and lend his name and presence to their circus.

Nathan Howes was joined by his younger brother

on both sides of the Atlantic. He had already had one career as the presenter of freaks and curiosities, most famously the diminutive Charles S. Stratton, whom he called 'General Tom Thumb,' as proprietor of the American Museum and promoter of Jenny Lind, the 'Swedish Nightingale' in North America. He had already made and lost fortunes and become notorious for the grandiloquence of his publicity: the 'Prince of Humbugs' was a title this all-time master of showbiz hokum gloried in.

As a lad, Phineas T. worked briefly in some capacity for Aaron Turner. The story goes that he did some clowning, but his job was mainly as a ticket seller. Later, in partnership with Seth Howes and Tom Thumb's father, he imported animals and set up a menagerie in 1851 which toured for four years. In 1860, having repurchased the museum, which he had sold five years earlier, he showed animals there, some of them performing tricks (his human exhibits were often performers too). It was not until 1871, after the museum had burned down for the second time, that he became a real circus proprietor. He was then 60 years old.

Dan Costello, a circus clown who had his own touring circus, and his partner and manager William C. Coup, a former roustabout and sideshow manager, together persuaded Barnum to become their partner in a new tented show launched under the all-inclusive if cumbersome title of Barnum's Great Travelling Museum, Menagerie, Caravan, Hippodrome and Circus. Coup became manager, Costello became director of amusements: he had experience as concessionaire as well as in the ring. Barnum invested money and provided his famous name and promotional genius.

The show opened in Brooklyn before going on tour. With three acres of canvas, it was the largest circus ever seen at that time, and in the first season grossed more than $400,000. The golden age of circus had begun! At first the company toured by wagon through New England and New York State, using the railroads to bring in audiences on special excursion trains, but soon changed to moving the circus itself by rail.

This was not the first circus to use the railroad: the Railroad Circus and Crystal Amphitheatre was operating in 1853 and, among others, Costello's own circus, the first to tour transcontinentally, had used the railroad. They played New Orleans in 1869 and after touring the South were working their way north when news came of the linking of the Union Pacific and Central Pacific tracks. One of Dan's partners, James Nixon, rode on the first through train and recommended that the circus make its way to Omaha and thence on the new line to Grand Island, North Platte and Cheyenne, Wyoming, with an extension by road to Denver.

The altitude and poor roads took a heavy toll of the horses and the elephants. When they moved on to Central City, Colorado, they had to leave a sick baby elephant

Seth in 1836. Seth then spent some time managing the Mabie Brothers Circus but in 1857, in partnership with 'Colonel' Joseph Cushing, formed a circus which they took to England. Returning in 1864, he renamed it Howe's Great London Circus and Sanger's Royal British Menagerie. Sanger failed to prevent this and other American circuses appropriating his name, but 'Howes' also became a much-used circus name.

It was not until 1871 that the name of P. T. Barnum entered circus history, although it was already well known

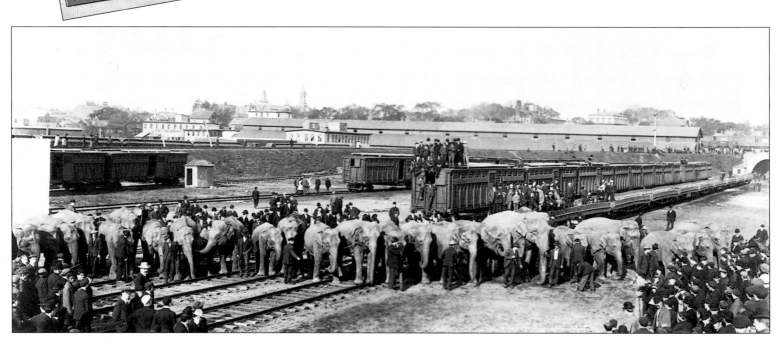

OPPOSITE TOP
Large circuses almost always toured a menagerie, which could usually be visited for an all-in ticket price. They included many animals in addition to those seen performing in the ring.

OPPOSITE BELOW
Elephants helped to haul wagons from the flatcars and to set up the tents, and crowds turned out to see them arrive.

ABOVE
In 1895, before the first silent film versions of Lew Wallace's novel Ben Hur, the circus was recreating the chariot race for its patrons, though the inclusion of a lady charioteer was circus licence. It remained a favourite circus spectacle.

LEFT
Barnum and Bailey presented William Showles and William De Mott so that patrons could judge for themselves which was superior. This kind of promotional gimmick was often employed by circus proprietors.

behind; it died two days later. After visits to Georgetown and Central City they entrained again at Cheyenne and went on to give performances in Utah and Colorado. At that point they sold the circus and decided to make their approach to Barnum.

At first the new circus used Pennsylvania Railroad cars but in 1872 Coup ordered their own flatcars, designed so that circus wagons could be ramped up and end-loaded with metal plates between each cart allowing them to be pulled along the entire length of the train. In 1873 the show expanded further, and so did its name, which became 'P. T. Barnum's Great Travelling World's Fair Consisting of Museum, Menagerie, Caravan, Hippodrome, Gallery of Statuary and Fine Arts, Polytechnic Institute, Zoological Garden, and 100,000 Curiosities, Combined with Dan Costello's, Sig Sebastian's and Mr D'Atelie's Grand Triple Equestrian and Hippodromatic Exposition'! The paying customers no doubt still thought of it as a circus. Two rings had been used in 1872 and now this 'Triple Exposition' adopted three, topping the two-rings advertised by Andrew Haight's Great Eastern Circus. In fact the third ring was simply the hippodrome track running around the other two: it was not until 1881 that the circus acquired three separate rings. Nor was it the first to do so. Lord George Sanger had three rings and two platforms when he set up on Plymouth Hoe in England in 1860, but Barnum set the pattern for American circus. In 1885, when Barnum and Bailey briefly combined with the Forepaugh show, there were four rings, plus two stages between them for acrobats, and the outer track around the lot! Some 40 years later Sells-Floto had five in the Chicago Coliseum and in the 1930s Ringling-Barnum regularly toured with a tented show containing three rings and four stages.

European circuses have sometimes used multiple rings, but the tradition of a single ring in a circular tent or auditorium has not been seriously challenged. It provides better concentration on an individual act. But European and American circumstances are different. Nineteenth-century European cities provided large populations from which to draw spectators, so that a circus could stay longer. Indeed, many cities could support a resident circus, and touring circuses did not have to travel such long distances between dates. Although small American circuses would continue on the road, moving frequently from town to town, the cost of dismantling, moving and setting up only made sense for a larger circus if the maximum takings were achieved at each performance, which meant drawing each audience from a wide area. This could only be achieved by increasing the seating, and that led to an oval or oblong arena in which several acts performed simultaneously in separate rings, enabling everyone to get a good view of the act nearest to them. It lost intimacy and focus but allowed magnificent spectacles to be staged, such as horse and chariot races around the encircling track, on a scale that a one-ring circus cannot equal. The tents became huge: from one that could seat 5,000 in 1872 the Barnum tent had increased to a capacity of 14,000 in 1898, and in 1924, at a performance in Concordia, Kansas, the show achieved a record of 16,728 spectators, although this included people seated on bales of straw around the hippodrome track.

Attitudes to scale and distance reflect the differences between the more closely settled European world and the wide open spaces of America. Even today many Americans will drive as far for a meal out with friends as some Europeans would only consider for their annual holiday. The experience of the spectator in each kind of circus will be different, but the acts must be of the same quality. In fact, they are often the same acts, for from the earliest days the greatest circus stars appeared internationally.

One of Barnum and Bailey's major rivals was Adam Forepaugh. Operator of a horse omnibus line in Philadelphia, he made an investment of 50 horses in the

The circus might have many clowns, and occasional real 'clownesses' as well as men in drag. Each had his or her own distinctive costume and make-up and many, as here, had performing animals as part of their act (though the duck and cockerel are also clowns)

Tom King and O'Brien Excelsior Circus and also had a licence to sell candy at a circus, before he bought the Mabie Menagerie in 1864 (it had been founded about 25 years earlier), and hired Dan Rice to front it. He then bought out O'Brien and launched Forepaugh's, which was the largest outfit touring by wagon in the early 1870s. He almost equalled Barnum in flamboyance and ran campaigns to discredit Barnum as a liar in his extravagant promotions, not that Barnum cared, for to him all publicity was good publicity and he even organized criticism of himself in the press to stimulate controversy! A major clash occurred over Barnum's 'white' elephant, Toung Taloung (which despite its billing was not white at all; Barnum himself probably felt cheated when he first saw it). Forepaugh's answer to this creature was to give one of his own elephants a coat of whitewash. After Forepaugh's death his circus was bought by James E. Cooper and James Bailey who in 1896 merged it with the Sells Circus, founded by the four Sells brothers in the 1870s.

A couple of years before Barnum became a circus proprietor, Dan Rice's circus had disembarked at the Mississippi town of MacGregor, Iowa, and fired the boys of the immigrant Rungeling family with the idea of circus. The five eldest put on a backyard show of singing, juggling, acrobatics and simple clowning, starring their goat, Billy Rainbow, with the eldest boy Al(bert) as ringmaster. The family moved to Baraboo, Wisconsin,

MEDIANS, IN A HODGE-PODGE OF QUEER ANTICS.

and from there in 1882, anglicizing their name, they produced a road show called The Ringling Brothers Classic and Comic Concert Company. The brothers numbered eight in total, led by Al, who had somewhere picked up experience as strongman, juggler and on tight wire and trapeze. It wasn't really a circus, but their initiative and enthusiasm attracted the interest of old-timer Yankee Robinson, whom Al had worked for. He agreed to join them, and in 1882 Yankee Robinson's Great Show, Ringling Brothers Carnival of Novelties and DeNar's Museum of Living Wonders set out on tour. Robinson died at the end of their first season but not before he had told everyone that in the Ringlings lay the future of American circus. His judgement seemed correct, for in the next few years they went from strength to strength.

Unlike some circuses, which fleeced their audiences and even encouraged pickpockets provided they handed over a percentage, the Ringlings ran an honest show. Because they did not perform on Sundays and laid down strict codes of behaviour for their employees they became known as a 'Sunday School' circus, although that did not prevent competitors from posting bills accusing them of being 'Thieves, Liars and Scoundrels. They Have No Show Worthy of the Name. They Sneak From Town to Town Under Cover of Darkness. They Plunder and Steal Even the Washings Hanging in Back Yards...'.

In 1890, with a dozen railroad cars, they toured small towns in the Midwest. The brothers no longer

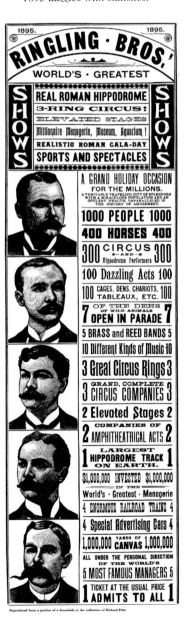

A Ringling Brothers advertisement of 1895 dazzles with statistics.

performed themselves. Al was equestrian director and producer of the show, Charles was general manager and organized touring arrangements, Otto handled box office and finance, John, who had been their clown, was in charge of railroad logistics, Alf T. public relations, Gus supervised advance postering and the youngest, Henry, saw the public in. In the mid 1990s they invaded Barnum's territory in New England and they went on growing. By 1897 they required more than fifty railcars.

Barnum died in 1891 but his partnership with Castello and Coup had disintegrated long before. Castello had retired and, after the end of the 1875 season, Coup, among other things unhappy with the way that Barnum let other companies use his name, went too. The Flatfoots operated the circus for Barnum until 1880, when he joined forces with one of his biggest competitors. James A. Bailey was a partner with James Hutchinson (and formerly James Cooper) in the International Allied Shows which embraced Howe's Great London Circus. The new partners celebrated with a great street parade in New York in March 1881, which featured 350 horses, 20 elephants, 14 camels, 4 brass bands and nearly 400 performers. Though Bailey himself temporarily withdrew from the business, he soon returned with a new contract that put him in total control and gave him half the profits.

In 1889 Bailey arranged to take what was now the Barnum and Bailey Circus over to England. It performed in London's Olympia exhibition hall before the royal family, political leaders, church dignitaries and thousands of the populace. Barnum once again met Queen Victoria and the Prince of Wales, to whom years before he had presented the young Tom Thumb. Another company continued in America, while Bailey remained abroad for five years. By the time he returned, the Ringling Circus had become a formidable competitor. He countered by expanding his own show, but the cost of competition was becoming excessive. Bailey still owned part of the Forepaugh Circus and in 1905 he sold half of his interest to Ringling's, passing its management over to Henry Ringling. Then Bailey died and in October 1907 Ringling's gained the whole Barnum and Bailey enterprise for $410,000, at the same time acquiring full control of the Forepaugh-Sells Brothers Circus.

After a time Ringling's closed down Forepaugh-Sells, but they kept the Barnum and Bailey and Ringling's circuses going separately, touring in different territories so that they were not in competition. The only top circuses which could be regarded as serious rivals were Sells-Floto and Hagenbeck-Wallace, though there were about ten other railroad and 30 smaller wagon shows touring in the States. Sells-Floto had been set up by the owners of the Denver Post and originally named the Floto (after their sports reporter) Dog and Pony show, but when a nephew of the original Sells brothers became its director it was renamed the Sells-Floto Circus. Ben Wallace, a proprietor with a reputation for extreme ingenuity in devising ways of fleecing the public, set up his circus in 1884 and in 1906 bought out the circus of a German proprietor, Karl Hagenbeck, established two years earlier in America and currently failing. The German was unable to stop him using his name so the circus became Hagenbeck-Wallace. After passing through the hands of several proprietors, in 1923 it became, along with Sells-Floto and most others that were not in the Ringling empire, part of the American Circus Corporation. Not long afterwards, however, the Ringlings bought the Corporation.

In 1883 William Cody, known as Buffalo Bill since the time when he supplied buffalo meat for the workers building the Kansas Pacific Railroad, launched his Wild West, Rocky Mountain and Prairie Exhibition. It opened in Omaha, Nebraska. Though a touring show, it was not a circus, but presented real-life cowboys and 'Red Indians', recreating their battles and stage-coach holdups along with demonstrations of trick riding and shooting in an outdoor arena where as many as 300 horsemen rode in en masse.

Cody had also been a scout with the Union Army in the Civil War and fought in the Native American wars from 1868 to 1872, earning a Congressional Medal of Honour during an engagement on the Platte River. His story was novelized by Ned Buntline and then dramatized as *Scouts of the Prairie* in 1872 with himself playing the lead. He worked as an actor for some years, then rejoined the US Cavalry as a scout in 1876, serving under Custer, before starting his Wild West Show. In 1885 the female sharp-shooter Annie Oakley joined his troupe.

Buffalo Bill toured widely in America and took the show to Europe, appearing before Queen Victoria, though after two decades of success public interest began to wane. There were imitators, including many circuses which added a 'Wild West' presentation as an aftershow or featured cowboy acts, later circuses featured such early Western movie stars as Tom Mix.

The First World War brought shortages of labour and transport and other problems, and a worldwide influenza epidemic added to the difficulty of keeping circuses going. Eventually, in 1919, Ringling Brothers and Barnum and Bailey were consolidated to become the largest circus in the world.

Whether by wagon or by rail, taking a large American circus on tour, together with its side shows, menagerie, stabling, dressing, kitchen and dining tents, was an exercise like moving an army, and it required a similar discipline. First, an advance party was sent ahead to publicize the show. The big shows had their own railroad car equipped with long tables down each side, poster stores above them, bunks below and a room to mix paste with its own water tanks and boiler. If there was close competition, a second team might go out to replace torn posters and cover the opposition's bills with their own.

When a big circus arrived, usually round about 5 a.m., the first thing to go up was the cookhouse tent. The big top might be on a second train arriving an hour or so later, while the cooks were getting breakfast, and seating came on a third train, another hour later, when all the stakes had been driven in and the tents were going up. Finally, the last train arrived with the performers at about 8.30. The animals were installed in the menagerie, seating was erected, the dressing tents and sideshows set up, while the aerialists checked their rigging, especially if others had installed it. At 11.30 all was ready and, after lunch was served to the company, the circus opened to the public at 12.30, with the first show starting at 2.15. Sideshow workers ate during the performance, and when it was over every one else was fed, usually about 5.30. As soon as supper was over the cookhouse, first to go up and first to come down, was dismantled and packed on the train. The sideshows and menagerie started to come down during the performance in the big top, and most of the remaining tents had gone by the time the performance ended. Even as the audience was leaving, the dismantling of the big top began.

The roustabouts, the men engaged to do the toughest work, were often a rough lot requiring firm discipline. Part of their wages was often held back until the season ended to ensure that they stayed on, and there were accusations of 'red-lighting' – throwing men off trains to avoid paying money owed to them. The victims, if they survived, saw the red tail lights disappearing up the track. The performers, who might already be appearing in more than one act under different names, were often expected to pitch in and help get the circus on the road. Proprietors preferred circus folk who could put their hand to anything.

For wagon shows, continually on the move, life was particularly tough. Sleep was taken where and

Ringling North assumed the management and he succeeded in paying off the debts. He also updated the circus, though not everyone liked his changes, feeling that circus was becoming too theatrical and losing its traditional appeal.

European circuses suffered heavily during the 1914-18 war. Besides the more obvious problems, horses were often requisitioned by the army. The French circus had flourished as a fashionable diversion and the German circuses of Renz and Hagenbeck were well established in

when it could be snatched. In a smaller circus show the family owning the show would probably have a horse-drawn living wagon, but grooms and performers might have to doss down in tents, stables, or under wagons, unless they were making enough money, and staying long enough in one place, to make use of hotels and lodging houses. The modern living caravan, now home to most travelling circus folk, is a comparatively recent development.

Circus life then (and now) was not all spangles, bright lights and applause. Anyone drawn by the superficial glamour and excitement to join the circus soon finds that it demands hard work and dedication. But the crowds that rushed out to line the street as the circus paraded through the town naturally gave no thought to the mundane affairs of organization. The parade itself was spectacular free entertainment. Elephants, horses, cage wagons with lions, tigers and other wild beasts, band wagons, the exotic circus folk and, bringing up the rear, the calliope playing its raucous tunes – from the 1880s through to the 1920s the parade was the ultimate advertisement.

But by the 1920s the growth of city traffic made such parades impracticable and, more importantly, the economics of the circus made them an extravagance that could be ill afforded. Good advertisement they might be, but after seeing everything for free would people dig into their pockets to buy tickets for the actual show? Some smaller American circuses still held street parades up to the Second World War, but the larger ones disappeared in the early 1920s.

The Depression that followed the Wall Street crash of 1929 imposed more problems. Box-office takings tumbled, and even the Ringlings were in serious trouble. After John Ringling's death in 1936 his heirs wrangled over the succession, but eventually his nephew John

Captain Jack Bonavita with 13 out of the 27 lions he trained for Frank C. Bostock's Jungle Arena in New York, one of a number of wild animal shows at the turn of the century. The gentling technique of training wild animals was pioneered by the German Karl Hagenbeck. Hagenbeck, an animal dealer, trainer, zoo owner and circus proprietor, did not have great success in America, but his circus remained one of the most important in Europe. Hagenbeck-trained acts, such as these lions, also appeared with many other circuses.

OPPOSITE
In the early days it was European circuses that went to America, but soon American circuses were travelling to Europe. Barnum and Bailey's toured for several years in Europe following their first visit to London. This German poster dates from 1900.

Raising the Big Top

*A*t first tents were supported on a central pole, the king pole, right in the centre of the ring. Using two (or more) kept the ring space free. Quarter poles were introduced later. They were set at an angle of 35 degrees to support the canvas on its downward slope. They had a prong at the upper end that slipped through grommets in the canvas, reducing sag and water pockets and allowing higher banks of seats. Side poles might support the outer perimeter where a vertical 'wall' of canvas completed the enclosure. Guy ropes or wires kept everything in place; they had to be carefully tensioned to ensure stability.

In the 1900s mechanical stake drivers began to replace the roustabouts' sledge-hammers, and in 1911 William Curtis of the Sells-Floto invented a wagon which spooled tent canvas off a roll where it was needed. Tent poles were trunks of Oregon pine or similar timber 50-70 feet (15-21 metres) long, the heavier bottom end becoming the top of the pole. Nowadays they are sections of aluminium that can be sleeved prior to set-up. Two methods have traditionally been used for hauling up large circus tents. The simplest, based perhaps on military traditions and also used for smaller tents, is the push-pole method. More favoured for large tents is the bale ring, derived from techniques used on old sailing ships.

In 1989 Johnny Pugh of the Clyde-Beatty-Cole Circus developed a method of using steel cable, connected to four centre poles, which could be winched up hydraulically in the manner employed on trawlers. Modern circuses increasingly use sets of king poles in the form of metal lattices with a ridge bar from which is suspended a cupola to which the plastic (no longer canvas) tenting is attached.

In the bale ring method, centre, quarter and side poles are all laid on site, with toe-pin stakes to mark position and prevent sliding and a bale ring slipped over the base of the centre poles. This is a spoked steel ring 1-3 feet (30-90 cm) in diameter to which canvas and aerial rigging are laced later. A heavy block of wood with a rounded bottom, the 'mud block,' is attached to the base: it allows the pole to roll and not sink into the ground as it is raised. Cable and guide lines are then lashed on and canvas unfolded, or the spool truck distributes canvas around the site. Men, elephants or tractors then haul up the king poles which provide leverage for raising all the rest. The canvas is attached to the bale rings and hauled aloft.

In the push-pole method, poles are laid on the ground, canvas spread over them and the sections laced together before being attached to the centre poles. Bale-rings may again be used to simplify attachment of rigging and to give ventilation space. Pronged side poles are inserted through grommet holes and then elephants, horses or tractors haul on cables to 'shoot' the base of each centre and quarter pole into place. As the canvas rises from one end, the crew works its way down its length, tugging on guy lines to tighten them and lashing them into place.

Parade Wagons

*T*he elaborate wagons designed for the circus parade had their origin in Britain and were first seen in America when Seth Howes brought some back from Europe in the second half of the 19th century. The Ringlings' first was an old dray with an eagle and a tin mirror on either side carved by their cousin Henry Moeller, and there were other specialist works such as Sullivan and Eagles of Peru, Indiana; Fielding Brothers and Sebastian Wagon Works of New York and Bode Eagon Works of Cincinatti. Working wagons were unadorned but parade wagons became increasingly elaborate, including floats representing continents, allegorical figures and fairy-tale characters such as Cinderella, with her glass slipper, and Prince Charming.

When John Ringling closed down some of the circuses the Ringling Brothers owned he had many of their wagons burned so that they should not fall into other hands and add to the attraction of their parades, and when the street parade ceased many wagons fell into disrepair. However, in recent times they have been collected and restored in the circus museums of Sarasota, Florida, and Baraboo, Wisconsin. Each July wagons from the Circus World Museum at Baraboo can be seen in a two-hour parade in Milwaukee, where the pictures seen here were taken.

LEFT
The calliope, the steam-powered pipe organ, usually came at the end of the parade, as there was always a risk that its boiler might blow up!

RIGHT TOP
The 'Whiskers' cage wagon, named for the bearded figures which guard its corners. It was built over 110 years ago.

RIGHT CENTRE
The United States bandwagon, built in 1903 and paraded by Ringling Brothers. Bandwagons were also used for transporting luggage at other times.

RIGHT BELOW
The Great Britain bandwagon was built for Ringling Brothers Circus in 1902 by the Bode Wagon Works in Cincinatti, Ohio.

FAR RIGHT TOP
This wagon, surmounted by twin lions, was originally made for the English circus of Lord George Sanger. It was bought by the Sir Robert Fossett Circus and obtained from them by the Museum. Each layer telescopes down inside the one below. Forepaugh had one similar, which Ringlings acquired in 1890 and used until 1918, removing figures of St George and the Dragon to make way for bandsmen's seats.

BELOW
The Ringling Brothers street parade of 1898 features a great number of themed sections. Though the numbers shown here in each may be exaggerated, such parades could take an hour or more to pass a viewing point.

ABOVE
The Lion's Bride bandwagon originated in the Karl Hagenbeck Circus (1905-06) and was used by the Ringling Brothers and Barnum and Bailey Circus as recently as the 1940s.

the early years of the century, but in Britain many acts transferred to the music halls and variety theatres, which paid higher wages than circuses could afford. Almost all the permanent circuses in Britain disappeared, though Sanger's and some others kept going. The largest circuses were mainly overseas visitors such as Barnum's and Hagenbeck's, which appeared at London's Olympia exhibition hall.

Some British entrepreneurs mounted shows

The Forepaugh and Sells parade for their New York season in 1900.

FOREPAUGH & SELLS BROTHER

GREATER NEW YORK'S GREETING AT THE DEWEY ARCH TO THE GLORIOUS

especially for Olympia. In the first season after the war the directors of the venue were entertaining a friend, a carriage builder and omnibus proprietor called Bertram Mills, newly returned from the war. They asked his opinion of the show. He made some diplomatic response but, when pressed, declared: 'If I couldn't do better I'd eat my hat!' A prophetic remark. The directors had no booking for the following winter and invited Mills to run a seasonal circus for them. He had no professional

GREAT SHOWS
CONSOLIDATED

RAGON OF ALL PARADES.

A circus parade down Main Street, Goldfield, Nevada: the real thing in a small town.

BELOW
A riding lesson at Sanger's Circus. A member of the public tries his hand at riding skills in 1884. He is strapped into a riding machine or 'Mechanic' invented by an American, Spencer Q. Stokes, for training riders. It had already been used for at least a decade and a half to get a laugh at the expense of a volunteer from the audience. The spar swings around with the central pole and the cable loops over pulleys where the operator must maintain control to ensure the rope takes the weight if the rider falls. A similar kind of device is sometimes used for aerialists and leapers.

knowledge of circus, but he knew horses and had once met John Ringling at the New York Horse Show. He arranged for Ringling to provide the circus for him but stipulated that Ringling must find his own transportation across the Atlantic, since British shipping had been decimated in the war. In June Ringling cabled to say he was unable to get shipping space and must ask to be released from his contract. Mills had to put his own circus together. In the immediate aftermath of war, the difficulties were even greater than normal. For example, he was unable to book German artists who were still excluded as hostile aliens.

In spite of the problems, Mills accomplished his assignment with great success. The Bertram Mills Circus became an annual event in London, and in 1928 Mills and his sons decided to launch a tenting circus. After carefully studying the way European circuses were run and working with the Great Carmo Circus in 1929, they launched it in 1930. It became the biggest of British circuses, joining such long-established family concerns as Sanger's and the Fossetts.

TWO
Circus Acts and Their Performers

A huge variety of acts have appeared in the circus ring, from solitary conjurers and jugglers to theatrical spectacles involving hundreds of performers and animals. Some have drawn an audience by the novel or exotic nature of the acts. Others have relied on audience participation: there have even been competitions in log-cutting or assembling machinery. Acts that endure demand skill, artistry and courage. Their range is far too wide for every type to be described, and the account that follows is restricted to the most typical acts and the most outstanding artists. Many performers, of course, combine a variety of skills such as juggling and acrobatics, or have specializations like knife-throwing within a riding or clowning act.

Elephants presented by Louis Knie Junior lined up in a grand mount at the Austrian National Circus.

RIGHT
A 1954 poster when Billy Smart's Circus featured polar bears and Himalayan black bears. Television appearances helped establish the reputation of this circus.

Horse Acts

It was the 18th-century riding masters and their tricks that brought the circus into being, and horses are still at the heart of all traditional circuses; indeed, some would claim that without horses there can be no circus. Today's equestrian acts can be divided into three broad types: *voltige*, in which a rider vaults on to and off a horse's back, together with trick riding in which the rider performs pirouettes and acrobatics on horseback or forms pyramids with other riders, often across several horses' backs; *haute école* ('high school') in which the horse performs manoeuvres in response to subtle signals given by body pressure or slight movement of the reins, as in dressage and *haute école* horsemanship; and liberty horses. *Haute-école* riding and liberty horses were not features of the earliest circuses but *voltige* and trick riding were there from the start, as was Astley's 'Learned Horse,' Little Billy, which had been trained to wash its feet in a pail of water, fetch and carry tea-making equipment, take a kettle from a fire and bring other things on request.

Some of the earliest *voltige* and trick acts have already been described: standing on the saddle, balancing on one leg in the 'position of Mercury', carrying another acrobat (often a child) standing on the shoulder, leaping on and off the horse, somersaulting on the horse's back and hanging down from the horse to pick up objects from the ground or swinging below the horse's belly to fire a pistol. The acrobatic manoeuvres became increasingly complex as time went on, as did the balancing acts, developing into a tiered pyramid of performers across several horses. A handbill in the Harvard Theatre Collection for a performance by Cayetano and Codet's circus in Boston, Massachussetts, shows three horses abreast carrying 14 riders: one sits on the saddle of the centre horse, two stand in the stirrups of each of the outer horses, one stands on the back of each; all except the pair on the outer stirrups carry others, the central figure standing and the others sitting on their shoulders. Similar displays have continued ever since. They require a matched position and pace from the horses as well as the riders' vaulting and balance skills to get into and maintain their position.

For the acrobatic rider a horse must have a level action and canter, the rise of its haunches helping to give a lift which the rider can use in launching leaps or somersaults from its back. At first, riders used the conventional saddles of their time. It was not until 1820 that displays were given bareback and two decades later this was still unusual. A wider and more stable base for horseback balancing and acrobatics was provided by a flat padded platform which replaced the saddle, an aid still used by some East European riders.

The early 19th-century riders would leap over garters (ribbons) held at a height just above the horse's head by clowns or others not otherwise involved. These might be several in number, and sometimes a larger sheet of fabric was used – a flag or banner, which by the middle

The liberty horses are a basic ingredient of the circus bill: Mary Jose Knie and her liberty horses.

of the century might be 9 feet (2.7 metres) wide, requiring a longer leap. An alternative was a balloon, not an actual inflated balloon but a hoop covered with paper which the leap breaks through, or a ring of burning kerosene or spirit-soaked tow. There have even been acts in which the horse jumped through the balloon and the rider leaped over the top of it. James H. Cooke developed an act in the 1850s in which, instead of leaping, he jumped on to a 40-foot (12-metre) long structure along which he ran, matching his timing to that of the horse below, so that he leapt back on to it just as it emerged at the other end.

The Richters perform an exceptional head-to-head balance on horseback in the 1970s. These Hungarians also performed with elephants in a springboard acrobatic act.

Somersaulting off a horse was being done in the 1780s, if not earlier, but Levi J. North, an American rider first encountered with the Quick and Mead circus in 1826, is said to have been the first to achieve a forward somersault on moving horseback when touring with Batty's Circus in 1839. Soon several other British and American riders had developed the skill. In 1846 North was doing it bareback, without the flat pad he had used previously. Though various riders built up the number of somersaults that they could do in succession, it was nearly 30 years before anyone managed a double somersault feet-to-feet on horseback. That was pioneered by another American, Robert Stickney. A later member of the Clarke family, John Frederick, achieved a double backward somersault in the early 1900s.

The backward somersault, usually done facing forwards, has to allow for the forward movement, unless the landing is made on a trailing horse. American James Robinson was with Spalding and Rogers circus in 1856 when he first turned 23 consecutive backwards and forwards somersaults over sheets four feet (1.2 metres) wide. (He was the protégé of John Robinson, who taught him to ride). He stood only 5 feet 5 inches (1.62 metres) tall and performed equally well through paper balloons. A double back somersault on the same horse is not to be seen today, but Aleksandr Sergey of the Moscow State Circus did one from the shoulders of another rider back on to a trailing horse (but wearing a safety lunge).

Bareback acrobatic riding reached a later peak with another diminutive performer, five-foot-tall Mae Wirth. Beginning as a child rider in her family's circus in Australia, she was booked by John Ringling for Madison Square Garden in 1912 when she was only 16. A featured centre-ring artist with the merged Ringling and Barnum

and Bailey circus, she was billed as 'The Greatest Bareback Rider That Ever Lived', no mere hype but a verdict endorsed by those who saw her. Until 1929 she appeared in every Ringling season, playing vaudeville dates in the winter. After that, she gave up one-night-stand touring and only accepted longer engagements, but she was still at the peak of her profession, as elegant as she was acrobatic, when she retired in 1938. Such skills were less frequent after 1945, though Martine Gruss was one exception.

The Cristianis had a great family bareback act in the 1930s. They would make a pyramid with eight people on five horses. Their great-grandfather, who was said to have been blacksmith to the king of Italy, took up tumbling as a hobby. His son, their grandfather, fell in love with a circus rider and joined her troupe, and his descendants excelled in several circus skills. They were already famous in Europe when Ringling invited them to America in 1934 but, when he refused them a solo spot with no performers in the other rings, they went elsewhere.

When they appeared at Olympia with the Bertram Mills Circus, their riding act included four brothers

OPPOSITE
*Mae Wirth, the diminutive Australian
acrobatic rider.*

simultaneously running and jumping to stand on a horse's back. One brother, Lucio, would leap from a standing position on to the back of a trotting horse to perform a series of backwards and forwards somersaults, then tie his ankles together with a handkerchief and repeat them. Another horse entered and followed the first around the ring and he somersaulted backwards on to it through a hoop; a third horse came in and all three circled neck to flank, then Lucio somersaulted back on to the third horse's croup. Among the many other brilliant things Lucio achieved was to somersault around a circle of horses landing on each alternate horse.

Another group, the Fredianis, in 1908, achieved an act in which they made a single column three people high on a trotting horse, probably the only act which could do this without the use of mechanics. The effect created such excitement and anxiety in the audience that on one occasion 18 people are said to have fainted.

Vaulting on and off horses, trailing from the stirrup and circling or clinging beneath their bellies came to be regarded as an exotic speciality of 'Cossacks'. Although the name may have been due to the costume rather than the origin of the performers, such performances did

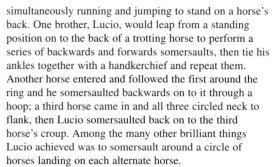

ABOVE
The Italian Caroli troupe bareback-riding pyramid at the Circus World Championships. The family was also famous as the Francescos clowns.

LEFT
The Nugzarov Troupe of 13 Cossack riders from the Caucasus, led by Tamerlan Nugzarov, with the Circus Knie.

indeed become a speciality of the Russian circuses. The excitement which they generate perhaps comes closest to the thrill that the first circus audiences must have felt at seeing trick horsemanship.

The clowning of the 'Tailor's Ride to Brentford', and variations on it, persisted as an act right through the 19th century, often making the tailor not so much incompetent as drunk. A variation in which the clowning led into a bravura display of riding began with the performer planted as an apparently drunk spectator clambering into the ring and attempting to ride a circus horse. The act was often known as the 'Flying Wardrobe' because, when the drunk manages to overcome the ringmaster's protests and is eventually standing precariously on the horse's back, he loses his coat, his trousers fall down, and then he sheds his many layers of clothing until eventually he is in his ring costume.

Mark Twain describes the act in *The Adventures of Huckleberry Finn*:

'... the next minute he sprung up and dropped the bridle and stood! and the horse agoing like a house afire too. He just stood up there, a-sailing around as easy and comfortable as if he wasn't ever drunk in his life – and then he begun to pull off his clothes and sling them. He shed them so thick they kind of clogged up the air, and altogether he shed seventeen suits. And then, there he was, slim and handsome, and dressed the gaudiest and prettiest you ever saw, and he lit into that horse with his*

WALTER L·MAIN

THE FASHION-PLATE SHOW OF THE WORLD

63 PERFORM IN ON

OVER **$50,000** OF BEAUTIFUL HORSES AND GORGEOUS TRAPPINGS.

A GRAND SIGHT.

Mr DUCROW as the BRIGAND.

Mr DUCROW as the GREEK CHIEF.

Andrew Ducrow in one of his character rides.

ABOVE
Yasmine Smart and her Andalusian
haute école *horse Bailaor at Monte Carlo.*

LEFT
Poster for Joe Berres' liberty-horse act with the Walter L. Main Circus.

whip and made him fairly hum – and finally skipped off, and made his bow and danced off to the dressing-room, and everybody just a-howling with pleasure and astonishment.'

Costume changes, as opposed to just tearing them off, were part of another act, though with the best performers it depended as much on skillful mime and impersonation, in which the rider assumed the appearance and character of a succession of different and often contrasting personalities. In the early 19th century Andrew Ducrow, who began his career as a rope dancer, performed all the kinds of act previously described, but he was especially celebrated for his mimes on horseback. At first he rode in static poses, but he developed these into continuous dramatic pantomimes. His many imitators' quick changes might present characters from Shakespeare's plays or well-known stories, stock

characters or national types, even symbolic personifications. Characters from the novels of Charles Dickens appeared even before their magazine serialization had been completed and were especially popular. A playbill for a ride based on *The Pickwick Papers* shows that they were closely modelled on the original illustrations by Phiz (Hablot K. Browne).

Another related ride appeared to present two characters on one horse, one usually carried by or on the shoulders of the other with a comic struggle going on. There was really just one rider; the head and arms of one figure and the legs of the other were dummies. Another clown act mounted the rider on the horse's back inside a sack, from which he struggled out, but when he emerged he had turned into a woman.

Ducrow's most famous act, first given in 1827, was the Courier of St Petersburg. It was copied throughout the 19th and early 20th centuries and recently revived by Katja Schumann at New York's Big Apple Circus. This symbolized the countries through which the courier passed with his message for the Tsar. He entered riding, standing astride two horses, a display known as the *Jeux Romains*, and as he continued to circle the ring a succession of other horses passed between his legs each bearing a banner representing a different country. As each passed he snatched up its white ribbon reins until he was eventually driving not two but six horses in pairs. Details included lying across the backs of the horses to represent his fatigue and relay stops. Some later performers increased the number of horses, the highest probably being a rider called Marin who in 1860 drove 15 horses, three abreast, in addition to the two on which he was standing, at the Paris Hippodrome.

Ducrow also presented the Ride of Mazeppa. The Mazeppa role had previously been performed by Master Astley at his father's circus in 1780, but its most famous interpreter but a genuine equestrian but a good-looking though rather second-rate American actress called Adah Menken. The act was based on the story of Ivan Mazeppa, the subject of poems by Pushkin and Byron. Mazeppa was brought up at the Polish court, where he seduced the wife of a nobleman. The husband caught him, strapped him naked across the back of a wild horse and sent it galloping madly away. Eventually it stopped near a Cossack camp and Mazeppa was released. He later became Prince of the Ukraine and a courtier of Peter the Great. The story was turned into a melodrama by H. M. Milnes in the 1860s.

A production at London's Royal Coburg Theatre
(later the Old Vic) was drawing poor houses when the
manager thought of replacing the actor playing Mazeppa
with the good-looking Miss Menken playing the male role
en travesti. Supposedly naked, though actually wearing
highly visible flesh-coloured garments, she drew in the
customers, and later repeated her success in New York. In
1864 Edward Tyrrell Smith, manager at Astley's,
provided her with an even more titillating presentation.
This was a full theatrical production, with the
noblewoman's seduction performed behind a gauze, and
the horse climbing through scenic crags for as long as
possible to extend the audience's view of the lovely Adah
strapped to its back.

At venues such as Astley's, equipped with stages,
there was considerable overlap between circus and the
equestrian drama. Horse episodes added exciting
spectacle to plays, but dramatizations appeared even in
small touring tent shows, too: the presentation of
highwayman Dick Turpin's ride to York and the death of
his horse Black Bess was popular in English circuses –
Sergeant Troy joins just such a circus to ride as Turpin in
Thomas Hardy's novel *Far From the Madding Crowd*. It
was still a feature on the Sanger's Circus bill in 1925.
Horses, of course, were a major element of the recreated
battles and attacks on coaches and wagon trains of the
Wild West shows, as well as featuring in displays of
rough-riding and roping.

A different kind of horsemanship was displayed in
acts based on the *haute école* or 'high-school' training of
horses. It originated in the training of cavalry horses and
formally choreographed horse 'ballets,' best known today
through the performances of the Spanish Riding School in
Vienna, which had been a feature of European court life
since the 17th century. 'Dancing' horses, were sometimes
a feature of early circuses. Astley presented a group of
eight in a cotillion and Ducrow showed a dancing horse
with wings strapped to its back which he called Pegasus.
It was in Paris, where the aristocratic associations of
haute école attracted the upper classes to the circus, that
equitation received its greatest acclaim. In 1833 Caroline
Loyo became an instant success on her first appearance at
the Cirque de Paris. François Baucher, who later
alternated with her on the programme, and his English
pupil James Fillis, became the greatest exponents of
haute école in the 19th century. Baucher had a rather rigid
style, the horse responding mechanically to his slightest
command, while Fillis produced a much softer and
more fluid effect. When Baucher was with Renz's
circus in Berlin he married Françoise Loisset and they
founded their own circus, but in 1855 his performing
career was ended by injuries received when a chandelier
fell on him as he was about to mount in the ring.
Fillis retired to take charge of the Russian Imperial

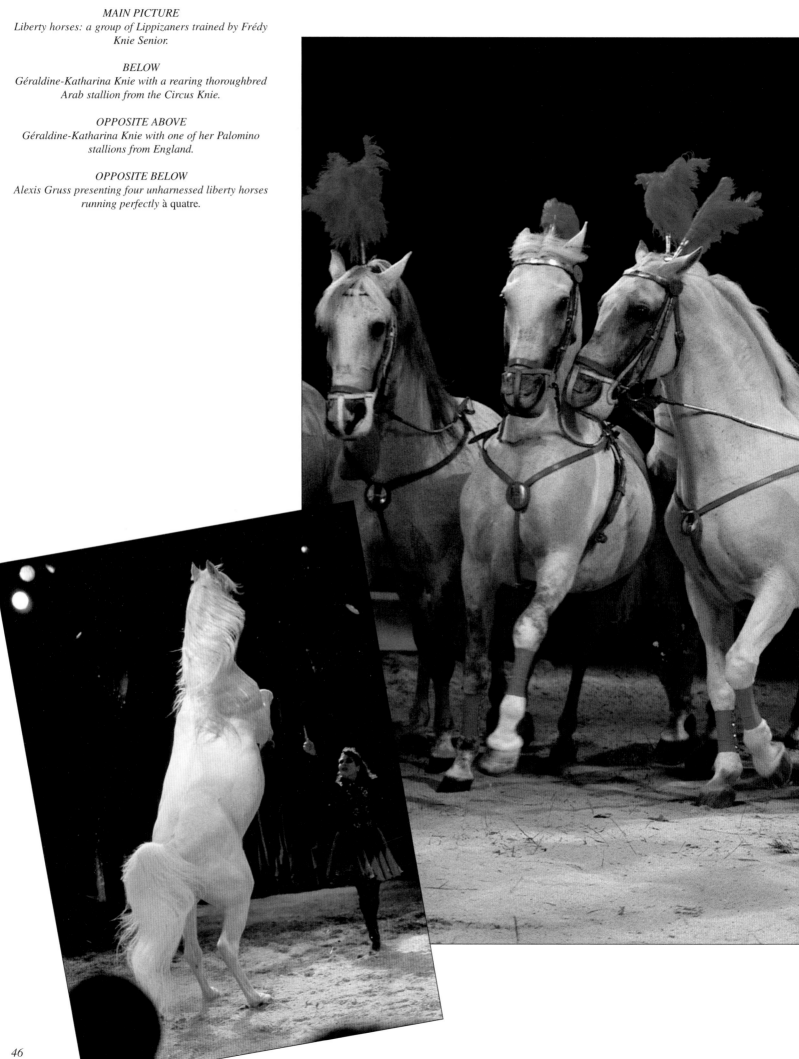

MAIN PICTURE
Liberty horses: a group of Lippizaners trained by Frédy Knie Senior.

BELOW
Géraldine-Katharina Knie with a rearing thoroughbred Arab stallion from the Circus Knie.

OPPOSITE ABOVE
Géraldine-Katharina Knie with one of her Palomino stallions from England.

OPPOSITE BELOW
Alexis Gruss presenting four unharnessed liberty horses running perfectly à quatre.

Cavalry School in St Petersburg.

Lady riders were the stars and the toast of Parisian smart society in the second half of the century. Some, like Anna Fillis, daughter of James, and Emilie Loisset came from circus families, but daughters of the bourgeoisie such as Elisa Petzold and impoverished aristocrats such as the Baronne de Rahden also found fame in the circus. Loisset and her sister Clotilde used to appear together but after a season starring at the Cirque d'Eté Clotilde married an aristocrat and Emilie continued alone, an aloof and dedicated professional until one day, her horse having refused a jump she whipped it, causing it to bolt and then, as it pulled up short, to fall backwards with her underneath. The horn of her saddle pierced her side and she died two days later.

Elvira Guerra, whose circus father had her riding a Corsican pony at the age of six, could ride the most unmanageable of horses. A high-point of her act with her *haute-école* horse Campeador was jumping over a banqueting table set with lighted candelabra – a feature echoed by Katja Schumann in her display at the World Circus Championships in 1978 with a leap over a table surrounded by champagne-drinking revellers.

Although most of these equestriennes rode side-saddle, wearing a formal riding habit, there were a few, such as Mlle Chinon, who rode astride dressed in male military uniforms. Even today, when the popularity of dressage competition at horse shows has provided new blood for the circus ring, Katja Schumann and some other equestriennes still ride side-saddle.

Haute-école training was important for what became known as 'liberty horses', which performed without a rider. Although individual horses reacting to their trainer's commands had been a feature since the earliest days, whole troupes of horses carrying out complex manoeuvres did not appear until the 1860s. They figured in the circus that Wilhelm Carré established in Amsterdam in 1854. Albert Schumann became one of the greatest trainers of liberty horses at the circus founded by his brother in Copenhagen, and through five generations the Schumanns have excelled in these and in *haute-école* acts. Frédy Knie Senior, and his son, also Frédy, and granddaughter Géraldine-Katharina have all trained and

OPPOSITE
Police and military horses learn to tolerate firecrackers, but for this 1909 act Jupiter and his rider had to maintain perfect balance while rising into the air.

The equine Blondin in 1887.

presented exceptional liberty routines in their Swiss circus. Other top trainers are Alexis Gruss in France and Mary Chipperfield in England. The Krone Circus in Germany have maintained fine liberty routines, while Enis Togni have a fine stud in Italy. In the 1960s, the German Franz Althoff presented no less than 48 horses performing around a hippodrome track. The large number made a spectacular effect though in style they were not comparable with the Schumanns or Knies.

Almost all circuses with animals have featured liberty horses, but none could rival the scale of such displays in America. In 1897 Barnum and Bailey were presenting 70 in a single ring, probably the largest liberty troupe ever exhibited.

The size of the big American circuses allowed even greater numbers of horses to appear with riders or in harness. In 1897 Barnum and Bailey advertised a cavalcade of 400 thoroughbreds, while 735 were said to have taken part in the spectacular Cinderella finale of their 1916 show. In 1874, Barnum presented chariot races in the Roman style in his Roman Hippodrome (later Madison Square Garden). In later years they became a feature of many of the large American circuses, sometimes as part of a great historical spectacular such as the *Burning of Rome in the time of the Emperor Nero*.

There have been many specialist horse acts, too. Blondin, a pony named after the famous tightrope walker, was with Forepaugh's Circus in 1887. He too, it appears, walked the tightrope. It was in fact a narrow plank painted to look like a rope, but it was still a considerable feat. In 1888-91, Forepaugh showed another horse called Eclipse, which on his trainer's command would spring from one swinging platform to another. He would then repeat the jump through paper balloons and rings of fire. There were also horses trained to keep their balance on a see-saw or, like Jupiter with Barnum and Bailey in 1909, to stand on a platform as it rose into the air, supposedly lifted by an air balloon, surrounded by exploding fireworks. The educated horses of the early days of circus which picked out the prettiest girl, did sums, or answered questions were unsuited to large circuses but occasionally still appear in smaller shows.

ADAM FOREPAUGH JR'S BLONDIN HORSE.

Ground or Carpet Acts

Chen Wenzui and Zheng Jianhui juggle and exchange ceramic pots.

The tumblers, jugglers and strongmen of the fairground and market place transferred easily to the circus ring. Because they work on the ground, often laying a carpet in the street or over the sawdust of the ring, they are usually known as ground or carpet acts, though weightlifters may sometimes make use of tent poles or ropes to demonstrate sheer lifting power without floor support.

Tumblers were performing prodigious leaps, somersaults and turns in the air, diving through hoops or clearing obstacles long before the first circus performances. Many circus artists combine some tumbling with their acts and the earliest riding displays included acrobatics. Conditions are of course different on horseback where motion makes control and balance more difficult.

Like many before him, Pablo Fanque, a black performer born in Norwich, England, whose real name was William Darby, was both rider and leaper. In 1836 he was leaping over the length of a post-chaise and the horses harnessed to it and then through a bandsman's drum before he landed. His successors performed even more extravagant leaps.

A leap can be performed unassisted, but even in pre-circus days greater power was sometimes obtained with a trampoline. This was not the modern gymnast's bouncing sheet suspended on rubber or steel springs, though that also found a place in circus acts from the 1880s, but a simple, short, wooden springboard. Alternatively, the performer might run down an angled line of planks to gain momentum and launch himself from an upward-sloping springboard, an apparatus known as a trampling board or *battoute*. Such aids made higher and longer trajectories possible, and circus performers were

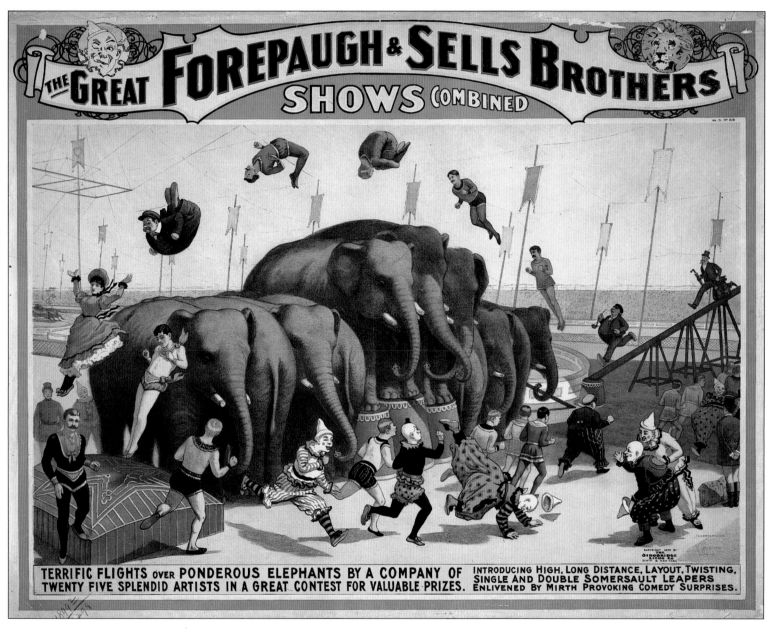

TOP
Sixteenth-century hoop jumpers.

ABOVE
*Forepaugh and Sells team of leapers
in 1899.*

always striving to cover greater distances over more challenging obstacles. A double somersault demands much more impetus at take-off to allow for the turns and a triple requires an elevation about one third higher than a double.

An exciting build-up was created by having a succession of tumblers leaping over an increasingly large number of obstacles, culminating with the star performer leaping the greatest length. It was further enlivened by different artists performing different kinds of leap, with twists and turns, and backward, forward and multiple somersaults, all enhanced by comic business and costume. An 1899 poster for Forepaugh and Sells shows just such a medley of clowns and acrobats leaping over no less than eleven elephants, three of them raised on rostrums, before landing on cushioning to soften their fall. The poster artist no doubt exercised some license and exaggerated the feat, though probably not the style and panache with which it was performed.

Tumblers have always been eager to take their skills a step further, and it is often difficult to say which performer was responsible for originating a particular act. A Mr Tomkinson has been credited with performing the first double somersault, in Edinburgh in 1835, although as late as 1868 Edward Hoyt, an American who was appearing as Buckskin Joe with Johnson's United Western Circus, claimed to be the first and sole exponent. It is difficult to believe that no one had turned doubles in the air long before Hoyt or Tomkinson, but both these men did it over the backs of horses. The following year Buckskin Joe and his brother Warren were doing the act with another circus over twelve running horses when Warren, having cleared the horses, failed to complete the second turn and fell against the ring bank. Landing on the back of a horse (or elephant) would have helped to break

Acrobats from India and southeast Asia were a feature of many circus bills, especially the Hagenbeck Circus, in the 19th century.

the fall but he was fatally injured. Later, Joe was to do a triple, but several others may have preceded him. Back in 1859 another American, Johnny Aymar, who had been with the Dan Rice circus and claimed to be first to do a double somersault over four horses, was working in England when in rehearsal he did a triple from the ground. Attempting it before an audience he turned only two and a half, landed on his face and was killed. William Hobbes was also killed attempting a triple at Astley's a few years later, and although the act may not look as dangerous as some others it is all too easy to break your neck. Among others, John Worland, after five years of sometimes achieving triples in rehearsal, eventually did one before an audience and official witnesses at Euclaire, Wisconsin, in 1881.

An act that was seen at Astley's first establishment was the pyramid, which can be built up with each tier of acrobats standing on the shoulders of those below or, less demandingly, on the thighs of the first row, which helps to lower the centre of gravity and increase stability. For an inverted pyramid, with the weight of all carried by the strongest member of the troupe, the aim is to balance the weight out to the sides, not to bear it all upon the shoulders. The still-unbroken record for the understander, as he is called, was set by Tahar Douis of the Hassani Troupe in the television studios of the British Broadcasting Company in Birmingham, England, in 1979. He carried a weight of 1700 lbs (771 kg) on his shoulders, made up of 12 men in three tiers. (By way of a change, he later took up wrestling with alligators!).

For vertical lift to carry the final acrobat, the topmounter, at the peak of a pyramid or column of others who have climbed up each other's bodies, or to land in a top chair or on a perch pole, a teeter board is used. This is in effect a see-saw, which is usually

operated by another acrobat jumping on the high end, although horses and elephants have been trained to provide the necessary impetus.

Balancing in a single column is more difficult than a pyramid but among those who achieved it four high were the Cristianis in the 1930s. Three of them mounted on each other's shoulders, then Benny stood on a teeter board while his brother Pilade jumped on the other end to send him into the air, landing upon the human totem pole made by his brothers. The Kehaiovi troupe at the Blackpool Tower Circus in 1986 probably exceeded all others with a column seven high, but they had the assistance of a support pole held between the acrobats to keep the column steady.

Balancing objects often depends for its effect on the awkwardness or unusualness of the object. Al, eldest of the Ringling brothers, is said to have balanced a plough on his chin. Performers can balance a pile of objects above them or climb the balanced stack as they build it and themselves balance on top, more and more being thrown up to them to increase the pile. Others have amazed audiences with their skill at balancing themselves upon just one finger, or on a walking cane held in one hand. An Austrian working under the professional name Unus did a finger act in Ringling shows of the 1940s and '50s dressed in top hat and tails and balancing on top of a globe-shaped electric lamp. Such acts are sometimes aided by wearing a glove which hides a brace to support the first knuckle joint, though that makes them only slightly less difficult.

A pole or other support can also be balanced by one acrobat to enable another to perform upon it. Louise and Daviso Cristiani had a pole act in the 1930s in which Daviso balanced the pole vertically on his shoulder while Louise climbed up it then placed her palm on its tip to

ABOVE LEFT
A member of Teresa Dourova's Russian troupe of acrobats somersaults up to an elephant's back.

RIGHT
The Chinese Hubei troupe perform their spectacular chair balance at the Circus World Championships in 1986. In the background a sculpture of an acrobatic posing act flanks the ring doors.

make a perfect handstand on one arm. Perch poles, either a simple pole or one with a horizontal top element, can also be held in a pouch supported by a belt. In one of the most impressive perch acts the Russian Kostiouk troupe in the 1980s used two shoulder-balanced perches. Having sprung to one, the topmounter then back-somersaulted to land on the other.

Other performers climb a ladder that is balanced to remain vertical with no support, among them the Russian Gridneff family act in the 1940s and '50s and a British artist who called himself Great Scott and dressed as a fireman. The Italians Leopold and Mario Medini did a head-to-head stand on top of a ladder and, with two ladders, supported a third person on their shoulders.

Modern perch poles of aluminium or lightweight steel are easier to support than the old wooden ones. Oriental performers often used bamboo, while westerners originally used heavy poles of pine.

The flexible steel pole known as the swaypole came into use early in the 20th century. It is secured at ground level and performers accomplish their manoeuvres at its perilously swaying tip. Fatalities have occurred when such a pole has snapped. One famous exponent was Fatini, who in 1980, aged 70, was still performing an act as a top-hatted drunk climbing to the tip of what must have been the tallest ever lamp post. His act was later taken over by another performer.

Many of the balancing acts done by a standing man have also been performed with the understander lying on his back and carrying or juggling objects or partners on the soles of his feet. Signor Colpi was doing this at Astley's in 1777, keeping as many as four children in the air. In the English-speaking world these are generally known as 'Risley' acts, after Richard Risley Carlisle, an American who excelled in a performance in

which he propelled his six-year-old son into the air to land on his father's feet, the child performing somersaults before landing. Because typically performed by father and son, these acts are also known as Icarian acts (after Icarus, in Greek mythology, who flew on artificial wings made by his father), or as Antipodean acts. Of the numerous objects employed in such acts, a barrel is perhaps the easiest to keep spinning with the feet, but all kinds of things have been juggled in this upside-down way, from poles to tables and fiery crosses.

The simpler Risley acts were sometimes performed on a rug directly on the ground, but they are greatly aided by a sloped support known as a *tranka* which is always used in modern circuses (and provides yet another generic name for such acts). An American called Derious was using one by 1843. One of the most spectacular acts was developed by Jules Lorch for his family troupe. He saw a Risley act balancing a barrel and, apparently without knowledge of any earlier Icarian act, thought of doing it with a smaller brother in the air. All the acrobats entered in bull fighters' suits of lights with whirling jumps and somersaults. Three then lay on *trankas* and threw the three smallest in Risley somersaults. For Ringling's Circus they appeared with a line of horses, somersaulting in sequence from the back of the first horse on to one man's feet, then over a horse on to the feet of the next man, over another horse and then, from the final

ABOVE LEFT
The ladder-balancing act of the Czech
Wolf family with the Circus King in
England in 1995.

ABOVE RIGHT
The Koziaks, a Polish acrobatic
troupe who, with their graceful flyer
Lydia, present a routine based around
this flexible pole, known as a Russian
bar. A Russian acrobat, Maxim
Dobrovitsky of the Egorov troupe, was
the first to perform a quadruple back
somersault in public working on such
a bar in 1989.

LEFT
The Chinese have become particular
exponents of foot juggling.

underman, in a double somersault on to the back of the
last horse. The climax was a column with the Risley
underman supporting two others, angled outwards, a
fourth sitting on them and three more standing on each
others' shoulders. Around them the horses raised one leg
on a pedestal and offered a hoof to be held by the two
horizontal men.

Heinrich Lorch, ancestor of Jules, had a travelling
show in the Rhine valley in the mid-19th century. His
son Louis ran away and worked in Paris, then on tour,
with a 16-year-old girl rider and two poodles. The act
eventually expanded into a circus with 100 horses,
while the versatile Louis developed skills as acrobat,
juggler, rope walker, strongman and clown. Louis's
children and grandchildren and four other acrobats
formed Jules's troupe.

More conventional juggling, with the hands rather
than the feet, is a very ancient skill. It has often featured
as an embellishment of other circus acts as well as an act
in its own right. In 1820 Ramo Samee, a juggler from
India, amazed British audiences by juggling four balls in
the air, but this soon seemed easy compared with the
skills of later artists. A little later a Frenchman, Henri
Agoust, was said to be a fine juggler, but in 1865 he
teamed up with the Hanlon brothers in Chicago and they
achieved greater fame as acrobatic clowns. A Hungarian
called Chenko was reported as juggling ten balls in 1903.

Prussian-born Emile Otto Lehmann-Braun began as a wire-walker and trapezist but after a bad fall found fame as Paul Cinquevalli the juggler. He took his professional name from his teacher, one of a trio of acrobatic clowns, Chiesi-Belloni-Cinquevalli. At first he dressed in Japanese style, for at that time, the 1870s, many successful jugglers were orientals. That fashion faded out in the last decade of the 19th century, and jugglers reverted to European dress. Later, the American Michael Kara, the 'gentleman juggler', wore evening dress and juggled his top hat, gloves, newspaper, cigar, matches and a coffee cup, but Cinquevalli was particularly renowned for a routine in which he juggled and rolled billiard balls around his body, catching them in special pockets in his green felt jacket, and gaining the name 'the Human Billiard Table'. He ended his act by catching a 48 lb (22 kg) cannonball on the back of his neck. Moritz or Morris Cronin introduced juggling with Indian clubs, which have since become a standard prop.

Others have added comedy by juggling the most incongruous mix of objects or even inviting the spectators to give them things to juggle. Eric van Arno juggled with a music stand, a drum and a cymbal in the 1950s. Cinquevalli sometimes worked with an egg, a bottle and a scrap of paper. Some have demonstrated their skill by juggling dangerous or unusual objects, even furniture. Fire juggling with burning torches looks more dangerous than it is but even billiard balls can be dangerous! At one performance by Cinquevalli a plate used in the act broke, cutting a finger to the bone before falling on his foot and breaking a toe. More obviously, juggling with double-bladed axes, as the Mighty Cradoc did for Sells Brothers, or with activated chain-saws, as American Dick Franco did in the 1980s, bring their own particular risks. Rudi Horn juggled on a unicycle or a see-saw on a cylinder, his speciality being cups and saucers which were finally landed in a stack balanced on his head, and topped off with a lump of sugar and a teaspoon. There are many other talented acts, especially those trained in the Russian circus schools. They produced Sergei Ignatov, who could juggle eleven rings faultlessly. Nevertheless, there have been few if any jugglers who could rival the Italian Enrico Rastelli.

Rastelli was born into a juggling family in 1897. His father owned a circus, and in 1909 young Enrico appeared dressed as a girl in his parents' aerial act. Rastelli senior wanted his son to follow him as director, disapproving of his wish to juggle (jugglers did not make

much money), but Enrico practised in secret, inspired especially by the skill of a Japanese juggler called Takashima. When his father discovered how good he was, the parental ban was withdrawn. He first juggled in the ring in 1915, at the Circus Truzzi in Russia, dressed in a kimono, but he is best remembered performing in a simple sports kit. He would routinely juggle eight or ten plates and was particularly renowned for his skillful manipulation and balancing of leather footballs. He finished his circus act juggling with flaming torches which he tossed almost to the circus top. He died young, in 1931, of blood poisoning resulting from infection of a cut made in his gums by the mouthstick on which he balanced objects. Rastelli is still the master, but a contemporary American, Anthony Gatto, is in the same high class; at only twelve years old he was performing similar routines.

Some circus jugglers achieved greater fame in other media. The film comedian W.C. Fields was originally a tramp clown who juggled cigar boxes. Eddie Cantor also was originally a circus juggler.

LEFT
*Modern strength juggler Markus,
from Austria, would include one
rubber ball among his metal ones. He
gave his audiences a shock by
bouncing this on his head and then
throwing it to the front row!*

RIGHT
*American Dick Franco juggling three
chain-saws, putting some 'buzz' into
his defence of the Circus World
Championship which he won twice.*

ABOVE
*Dr Hot and Neon with their
hat-juggling act. This American act
had its origins in street entertaining.
They developed into top performers
on television and had their own stage
shows.*

LEFT
*Russian Victor Philipovich juggling
clubs. He is manager of a Moscow
Circus touring unit as well as an
accomplished juggler.*

Plate spinning is a skill often linked with juggling. Plates can be tossed from stick to stick while spinning, spun on a finger, or passed around the body. It was never a major circus feature, except in Chinese acts, until the charismatic German Bartschelly made a big act out of it in the 1950s. He had dozens of imitators in circuses large and small. Chinese troupes often offer the spectacle of a dozen girls each with eight hand-held sticks, all bearing spinning plates.

Strongmen were a feature of the pre-circus fairs, and can still be seen giving street exhibitions, though it is not only men who have exploited their physical strength in this way. In New York as early as 1753 Mrs Dugee was an attraction in her husband Anthony's troupe, where she was billed as the 'Female Samson.' She could lift an anvil with her hair and would lie between two chairs with a 300 lb (136 kg) blacksmith's anvil on her chest while men

Strongmen Louis Cyr and Horace Barre performing, about 1898.

struck it with sledge hammers. Six men stood on her in the same position, an iron bar was broken on her chest, and when a stone of 700 lb (317 kg) was placed on her she could throw it off to a distance of six feet (1.8 metres). Or so it was said.

To make an impact in a large circus the act had to be fairly dramatic. At Cirque Rancy, France, Bernard Leitner broke chains by expanding his chest. He would also lie between two stools and support a horse upon a see-saw on his stomach. Bent backwards to rest on hands and feet, with a special board to spread the weight along his body, he could managed two horses on a seesaw! In the 1890s Louis Cyr, with John Robinson's Circus, was challenging all comers to match him as the 'Strongest Man on Earth', lifting 4,300 lbs (1,950 kg), supporting 25 men across his shoulders, or an elephant on his stomach (albeit a baby one). As support in his act he had the

French strongman Horace Barre. A German strong-woman, Catherine Brumbach, who became known as Catherine the Great, could juggle cannon balls of 30-50 lbs (13.6-22.6 kg) in 1916 when she was at the Wintergarten in Berlin. It was reported that, when she slapped the face of an admirer who dared speak to her in the street, the force of the blow hurled him through a café window!

Contortionists were another act that followed on from the fairground, though they were not called that until the mid-19th century. Technically, if they bend forwards they are 'posturers' and if backwards 'benders'. J. H. Walter, an Englishman who performed as Marinelli in the 1880s, wore a tight snake-like costume to make him appear even more sinuous and so became known as the Serpent Man. In America this was an act in which white audiences accepted black performers such as Marsh

GE FEATURE
E BARRE –

347 LBS.   347 LBS.

HORACE BARRE

RIGHT
Strongman Ivan Karl adopted a Russian persona for his act but he was actually Anthony Carrol from England. His short stature made his carrying of a 20-stone (127 kg) man from the audience above his head even more impressive.

RIGHT
Chinese plate spinning and balancing.

BELOW
The Luhoe troupe of juvenile contortionists, who continue the centuries-old Chinese expertise in acrobatics and contortionism.

Craig. Others included George Crawford and Billy 'the Human Frog' Williams. There are many currently from Mongolia. They need to be slim and cannot eat until they have finished performing for the day. Though many contortionists work solo, it is an act that is dwarfed in a large arena, where intertwining pairs or groups can often be more effective. Recently the Circus du Soleil have recruited and trained a group of four girl contortionists (Nadine Binette, Isabelle Chassé, Jinny Jacinto and Laurence Racine), which breathes new life into this kind of performance. They won a Gold Clown at Monte Carlo in 1992 with a difficult and cleverly choreographed act.

Walking on a rolling barrel or ball is another skill, usually combined with others when used on the ground, but globe walking has also been deployed up and down ramps and spirals. This kind of act was already being performed in the 1860s. Another act using a ball on a

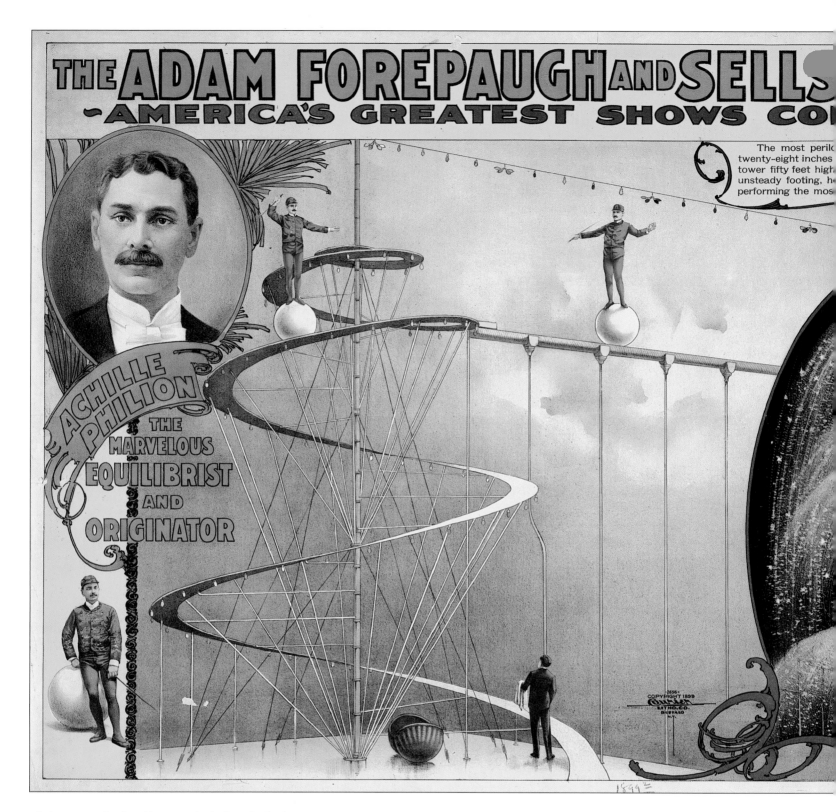

The most perilo
twenty-eight inches
tower fifty feet high
unsteady footing, he
performing the mos

ACHILLE PHILION
THE MARVELOUS EQUILIBRIST AND ORIGINATOR

spiral ramp was developed by contortionist Leon La Roche in about 1880, but this ball moved mysteriously on its own and hence was known as *La Bola Misteriosa*. It rolled up a spiral ramp and down again, then opened up to reveal La Roche inside it. Beginning with a ramp 12 feet (3.6 metres) high, he later doubled the height. The act was brought to an end when all his equipment was lost in the First World War but he was discovered by the German Circus Sarasani and persuaded to revive it though he was then 60 years old. Sadly, he was drowned when he jumped from a ship sailing from Australia to Spain. His act has been recreated by others and in the 1980s was performed by Geroku, though he reverses the presentation and begins by being put into the ball by an assistant.

Many other skills are seen on the ground in the ring from stilt-walking to roller skating. Speciality acts such as knife throwers or illusionists are sometimes presented and no doubt the circus will always find a place for new ones.

ABOVE
Achille Philion's spectacular globe act.

ABOVE RIGHT
Joseph Wallenda combined juggling and acrobatic skills with balancing on a ball.

RIGHT
Chinese 'lions' balance on rolling globes complete with a top-mounter.

FAR RIGHT
The Golden Pyramids, a posing act from the Hungarian State Circus. Though a major feature of circuses in the late 19th and early 20th centuries, displaying both on floats and on horseback as 'living statues', such acts are today more likely to involve acrobatic balancing.

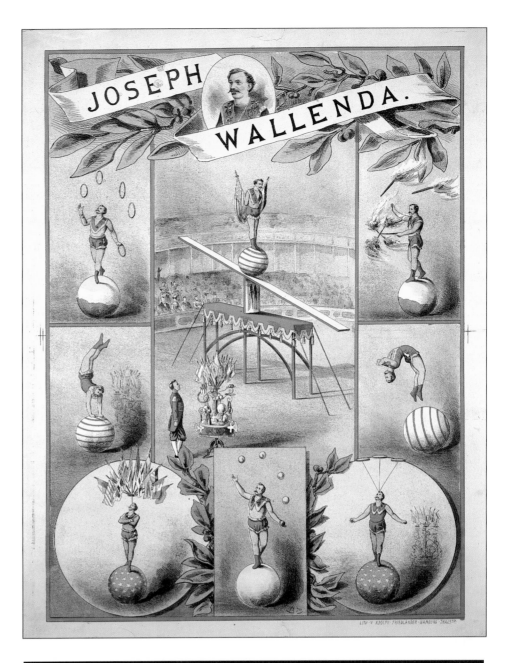

Rope and Wire Acts

An 18th-century French engraving of Mahomet Carantha, the Turkish rope dancer and equilibrist who taught Anthony Dugee, shown here on slack rope, tightrope (bottom left) and balanced ladder.

Rope walkers or funambulists, from the Latin term,
have been around since classical times, but the
pre-circus performers were essentially rope
dancers whose appeal lay in the grace and skill of their
steps upon the rope rather than their acrobatics. As circus
developed it demanded more challenging balancing feats
with increased handicaps and risk-taking spectacle.
Performances could be on slack rope, tightrope or, from
the mid-18th century on a wire, though stranded wire
cable was not available until the 1830s and hemp ropes
were certainly still in use even later than that. Indeed,
although we now speak of the high wire, reflecting the
5/8 inch (16 mm) steel-strand cable in general use,
tightrope remains the layperson's term.

The slack rope is kept taut by the weight of the
performer, who must keep it in position beneath his or her
centre of gravity. The head and shoulders maintain their
position whilst the legs are in constant movement pushing
the rope from side to side. This can be effective in
clowning but is more difficult than maintaining one's
balance on the less mobile tightrope. Yet, if a
contemporary French print is to be believed, at the end of
the 1740s Mahomet Carantha, described as Turkish, was
presenting headstands, juggling and balancing trays of
glasses on his forehead while propelling a wheelbarrow
with his knees, balancing a chopper on his nose and
carrying flaming torches – all on the slack rope. He also
played the violin on an unsupported ladder. A decade later
Carantha's former apprentice Anthony Joseph Dugee was
performing similar feats in New York.

On the tightrope it is his or her own centre of
gravity that the performer must keep over the rope or
wire. When the hands are not needed for other activities,
carrying a balance pole horizontally helps to lower that
centre of gravity and reduce sway upon the rope. Some
later female performers used a parasol: air resistance
helped to maintain balance, although with any gust of
wind or upcurrent of air at heights it could become
more of a drawback than an advantage. In contrast,
deliberate handicaps were sometimes introduced to
make the act more dramatic: chaining the ankles, for
instance, or wearing baskets on the feet (a feat which
trick riders copied).

At first, circus tightropes were usually not much
more than 10 feet (3 metres) from the ground. Later, with
large buildings and high tents, they could be rigged
higher, and outdoors, between trees or buildings, higher
still. French tightrope walker Marguerite Lalanne, known
as Madame Saqui, who appeared at Astley's in London in
1816, performed in the same season outdoors in Vauxhall
Gardens. Nearly half a century later Jean François
Gravelet, the celebrated Blondin, made his famous
tightrope crossing 160 feet (48 metres) above Niagara
Falls. Many spectacular crossings of rivers or between
architectural landmarks have been achieved by circus
performers. They require endurance and concentration but
no more skill than their circus acts, unless weather

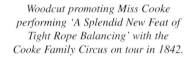

*Woodcut promoting Miss Cooke
performing 'A Splendid New Feat of
Tight Rope Balancing' with the
Cooke Family Circus on tour in 1842.*

*LEFT
Blondin's famous tightrope walk
across Niagara Falls.*

conditions increase the danger. In San Juan, Puerto Rico, in 1979, a gust of wind dislodged Karl Wallenda as he walked a wire stretched between two hotels and sent him to his death.

One elaboration in the early circuses was to use more than one rope, either side by side or one above the other, with performers on each, enhancing the drama of the rope dancing, mime and singing that were probably included. Multiple costume changes on the rope, like those on horseback, were also popular. Long before circuses started, female funambulists had sometimes cast off their skirts while on the wire to reveal legs clad in breeches, the better to display their skill, and even in the Victorian period ballet skirts, which revealed the ankle and lower leg, might be worn, or after 1850 varieties of bloomers .

Objects as well as people could be balanced on the rope. In the 1840s Miss Cooke was appearing with her family's circus sitting on a chair at a table – both balanced on the rope – pouring herself a glass of wine from a decanter. A century later Camillo Mayer presented a very similar act for Ringlings Circus though, more abstemiously, he drank coffee.

When and by whom the first somersaults were done on a rope or wire is debatable. One candidate is Abraham Saunders at London's Sadler's Wells as early as 1781, another is a Mr Wilson at Astley's in 1811, but the circus historian George Speaight suggests that these and several later references meant less than has been assumed, such as somersaults from rope to ground, or turns with an intermediate handstand, or ending in a landing with the rope between the legs. Publicity for Andrew Ducrow, a rope dancer as well as a famous rider, announced that he would perform a 'double Somerset' in the theatre at Bath in 1816, and in 1817 Wilson was billed to somersault while firing two pistols, which would prevent him using his hands.

What is certain is that both backward and forward somersaults were being done in 1841 by two of the sons of rope dancer and circus proprietor J. M. Hengler. On the rope or wire a forward somersault is the more difficult because in the turn it is impossible to see where the feet are going to land.

In the 1880s Ella Zuila, sometimes billed as the 'Female Blondin', had an act in which she not only walked the tightrope with baskets on her feet, as Mr Vilalliave had done in 1818, but walked with a sack over her head and body, stood on a chair, carried her husband on her shoulders, pushed her child in a wheelbarrow and poured water from one vase to another above her head. These were all feats performed by other early rope dancers, but she also rode a bicycle and, amazingly, walked the wire on stilts! Stilt walking on the wire has been done more recently by Manfred Doval and Roger Regor in the 1970s and '80s and by Freddy Nock and Lazlo Simet, among others.

'Bird' Millman, a favourite of the 1920s, was the first American woman to appear on the slack wire. She worked on a wire 36 feet (10.8 metres) long, twice the usual length at that time. Her performing name came from her tiny, bird-like steps along the wire, with arms extended to aid balance, and holding brightly coloured balloons. The Bird also sang while she performed. She made her debut in her parents' act but was performing solo by the age of twelve.

It was not until 1923 that a forward somersault was successfully performed on the low tight wire. This was done, after five years practice, by Australian-born Con Colleano at the New York Hippodrome, on his fourth attempt. Son of an Irish father and Australian mother, a dancer, he first appeared in public aged three being tossed on his father's feet in a Risley act. He began to learn the wire at ten. In Mexico and Spain he picked up some of the skills of the bull ring and Spanish dancing and incorporated these in his act. Entering in a costume recalling that of a matador, before mounting the wire he made a few passes with a scarlet cloak as though to a bull. He began his performance using the steps of the tango and traditional Spanish dance, matching if not surpassing the artistry of the early rope dancers. Then, in the middle of a backward somersault, he removed his outer trousers leaving him in silver breeches for the rest of his act, which climaxed in the forward somersault.

The Wallendas are a circus family of Austrian-Hungarian stock who have provided some of the greatest high-wire performers. Previous generations included jugglers, tumblers, an acrobat and an animal trainer, but as a boy Karl Wallenda worked in a coal mine in Germany during the First World War. At 16 he answered a newspaper advertisement for someone who could do handstands. To his surprise he discovered they had to be done on someone else's shoulders 40 feet (12 metres) in the air! Unfazed, he began his career with the German wire walker Louis Weitzman. In due course he moved on, forming his own group with his brother Herman and two other acrobats. They developed a high-wire act in which they stood on each other's shoulders to form a pyramid. They made their debut in Milan in 1922. Karl crossed the River Danube on a cable in 1923 and they first performed their three-high pyramid for Circus Gleich in 1924. The 'Flying Wallendas,' as they then called themselves, were performing in Cuba a few years later when John Ringling

offered them a contract. They opened in Madison Square Garden in 1928 and stayed with Ringlings until 1946.

The Wallendas developed several new high-wire pyramid acts. In one, two cyclists balanced a chair on a pole between their shoulders with another member of the troupe standing on the chair and a girl standing on his shoulders. Another arrangement had two walking on the wire, a bicycle balanced on a pole between them, a third man riding the bicycle and a girl standing on the cyclist's head. A third, first achieved in 1946, began with two pairs of men with poles between them; one man stood on the centre of each pole supporting another pole with a chair balanced on that and the girl this time standing on the chair. Supporting these spectacles were such 'routine' feats as synchronized headstands on the wire.

In 1970 Karl walked a wire 750 feet (225 metres) above Tallulah Gorge in Georgia. It took him a quarter of an hour to cross the 233 yards (210 metres) with a couple of pauses to do headstands. Six years later, in London to help judge the Circus World Championships, he did a walk at seventh-floor level between two wings of a hotel next to Tower Bridge. Two years later, aged 73, he was killed when blown from the wire in Puerto Rico.

The Wallendas, who formed two troupes to perform their acts, had more than their share of ring accidents and tragedies. In 1933 Willy, Karl's brother, was performing in Sweden with the second troupe when

LEFT
Joselito Barreda, from Colombia, whose presentation seems to be influenced by Colleano's style, skipping on the high wire. Skipping with ribbons was often a part of early wire-walking acts.

RIGHT
Con Colleano, who worked on the low tight wire. His acrobatics were placed in a context of rope dancing that linked directly with his distant predecessors.

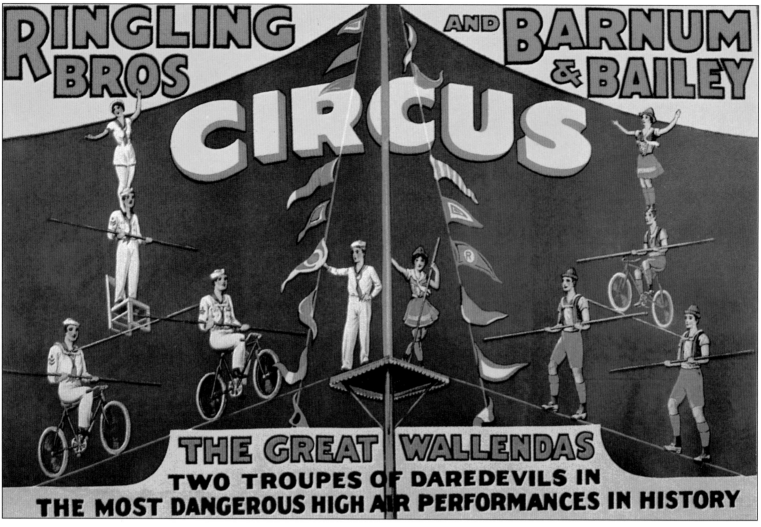

RINGLING BROS AND BARNUM & BAILEY CIRCUS

THE GREAT WALLENDAS
TWO TROUPES OF DAREDEVILS IN THE MOST DANGEROUS HIGH AIR PERFORMANCES IN HISTORY

the back wheel of his bicycle came off the wire and he fell. Though he landed in the safety net, he rebounded and was thrown against a wall, resulting in injuries from which he died. The following year Karl's troupe was performing with Ringlings in Akron, Ohio, when a guy rope loosened and the wire suddenly dipped. Karl dropped his balancing pole, dodging out of its way, and the ring staff dropped the safety net they were holding to avoid the pole. Herman managed to clutch the wire and get a leg over it while Joseph, as he fell, managed to grasp Herman's legs, and they scrambled along the cable to the end pedestal. Karl, who was on the top chair, also managed to grab the wire, but his diminutive wife Helen could not reach it as she fell from his shoulders. However, Karl managed to grip her between his legs and held on until the net was in a safe position for both to drop into it.

In 1944 they were performing at Hartford, Connecticut, when fire broke out in the tent. They reached the ground with only their costumes singed and though burning canvas fell on Helen she was not seriously harmed. On another occasion, in Nicaragua, there was a major earthquake while they were doing their act but they got down safely.

They were not so lucky attempting a seven-person pyramid at Detroit Coliseum in 1962. Karl's nephew Dieter Schepp and his teenage sister Jana had come from Germany after the Second World War to join the act. Dieter lost his grip on the balancing pole and fell, bringing most of the pyramid down. Jana was at the top and was caught by Karl and his cousin Gunter, but Dieter and Karl's son-in-law Richard Faughnan were both killed and his adopted son Mario left partly paralyzed by his injuries. Karl, despite his own injuries, which included a cracked pelvis, discharged himself from hospital and was back on the wire the next night, but he never again presented the seven-man pyramid. The following year

The Great Wallendas: troupes formed from Karl Wallenda's family and those he trained were predominant among high-wire acts for four decades.

RIGHT
The Wallendas in a three-high version of their act with bicycles and a chair, and (above, clockwise from top) Joe Geiger, Herman, Helen and Karl Wallenda.

OPPOSITE
A three-man bicycle pyramid by the Quiros, a Mexican high-wire troupe featured in top circuses such as Ringling, Knie, Enis Togni and Arlette Gruss and probably the best and most dramatic of current high-wire acts.

Helen's sister, who was not part of the act but performed herself as Miss Rietta, was also killed, falling from the wire in Omaha, Nebraska.

Another generation of Wallendas maintain their circus tradition and high standards. Among them is Tino Wallenda Zoppe, whose act with Circus Flora includes walking down the anchoring cable to the ground without a balance pole, a skill rarely seen today though done by some of the early wire walkers.

An artist who walked up an inclined wire was Harold Alzana. Born Harold Davis in Yorkshire, England, he became a coalminer as a lad, performing with his sisters in his spare time – and working seven shifts a week during the Second World War while developing his skills. He used to incorporate a number of faked near-falls in his act to heighten audience excitement, but he also had a number of serious genuine ones. The Alzana's family act, which included his wife, had many echoes of the Wallendas, but one speciality was a bicycle with a trapeze suspended from one wheel. Harold rode the bicycle on the high wire while his two sisters performed below him on the trapeze.

Oklahoma-born Hal Smith ran away to join the circus at 14 and became professionally known as Hubert Castle, adopting an English persona. He worked on the bounding wire, which has a spring at both ends to facilitate somersaults, and would also do handstands on the wire and ride along it on a unicycle. His first partner Bunny Dryden, was another victim of a fall from the high wire.

A Russian group, the Solokhin Brothers, achieved a four-high column on the high wire in 1962. Another Russian act, the Ahmed Abakarov troupe, went three high with one acrobat standing on the first man's shoulders and the third balancing on one hand on the second's head. Their act climaxed with a girl on a three-high column somersaulting backwards on to the shoulders of another man standing on the wire behind the column.

Perhaps the most famous high wire-walk since Blondin crossed Niagara took place in 1974, when Philippe Petit contrived illicitly to stretch a wire between the twin towers of the World Trade Centre in New York, shooting it across with a bow and arrow. Born in Nemours, France, in 1949, he had become a street juggler and magician. He began to wire-walk at 17 and at 19 wrote a play about wire-walking. In 1969 he wire-walked across the Seine, then between the towers of Notre Dame cathedral in Paris and over Sydney Harbour Bridge. His New York exploit resulted in his arrest and he was charged with trespass and disorderly conduct. The judge gave him an unusual sentence: to put on a free show for children in Central Park. He made his debut with Ringling and Barnum and Bailey at Venice, Florida, in 1975 but four days later slipped and fell, breaking his wrist and a rib, and so missed the New York season's opening, though he rejoined the show at Madison Square Garden a few months later.

The Flying Trapeze

Acrobatics on the bar were originally performed only on stationary apparatus, but about the middle of the 19th century suspended bars were introduced. Acrobatics on a trapeze by one or more performers can be very effective. Multiple acts usually involve one artiste suspending others, sometimes using an 'iron-jaw' mouth grip, balancing with chairs and other properties as on the wire. However, it is acts on a swing trapeze, in which the artiste lets go of the trapeze and swings freely through space to another trapeze, or to be caught by a partner on another trapeze, that generate the most excitement. They have become perhaps the highlight of a circus performance.

Trapeze 'flying' was the idea of Jules Léotard, whose father ran a gymnasium in Toulouse, France. He developed the skill of swinging on one trapeze and flying through the air to catch the bar of another. He is said to have practised over a swimming pool. He was studying for the legal profession, but his trapeze work was seen by visitors connected with the circus, and in 1859, when he was 21, he was invited to display his skill at the Cirque Napoléon in Paris. He was soon launched on a quite different career. His father assisted in his act by setting the empty trapeze swinging from one platform as Jules launched himself on a trapeze from a platform opposite. A long mattress was laid beneath in case he should fall. He added a somersault between the trapezes and in 1860 he was doing a 27 foot (8 metres) air jump at the Renz circus in Berlin.

Léotard had a sensational success when he appeared in London at the Alhambra in 1861. Soon, English music halls were celebrating the trapezist in a new song, words by Gaston Lyle, music by George Leybourne:

He flew through the air, with the greatest of ease,
This daring young man on the flying trapeze;
His movements so graceful, all girls he could please
And my love he purloined away.

Sadly, his career was short, for he died of smallpox in 1870. Although few people today have ever heard of Léotard, his name is commemorated in the close-fitting body garment he wore, now widely used by dancers and acrobats.

Léotard had English imitators, James Leach and Richard Beri, who were featured at the Alhambra a year before he went to England, after developing their act in Russia. There was also a woman trapezist in action by 1868 but, while Jules did a somersault between trapezes, all Mlle Azella could manage was a turn as she dropped from trapeze to safety mattress.

It was not long before others were performing multiple turns: Thomas Clarke, who appeared as Niblo, Onra and Bonnaire were all three doing doubles in 1869, and within a few years the Frenchman Edmond Rainat and his brothers Jules and Alexis were doing them too.

OPPOSITE
Sabu in his trapeze act which
includes balancing in and
handstanding on the solo trapeze.

BELOW LEFT
A poster for Barnum and Bailey's
Circus on tour in Germany, issued in
1900.

RIGHT
Terry Lemus at the start of her triple
somersault to brother Jim, who is
waiting to catch her.

The act was taken a stage further with the introduction of a catcher about this time. In one well-documented act an English girl working as Mlle de Glorion leaped from the trapeze through two paper balloons into the waiting hands of one of her male partners.

Another lady trapezist, Lulu, was doing a triple somersault in 1871 but, like Mlle Azella, not to the catcher or trapeze. She was also shot from a cannon to the trapeze on the same bill. In fact 'she' was a young man who continued to appear as a girl for many years and was the first artiste for whom there is documentation of a safety net, replacing the mattress.

The Rizarelli Brothers, another group appearing at the same venue, the Holborn Amphitheatre, that year launched the flyer from a springboard rather than from another trapeze.

Another innovation around 1870 was the trap head stand, a small cup introduced by American Keyes Washington, which enabled a stable headstand to be performed on the trapeze. Still used, it helps distribute weight and give support in a lateral as well as a forward and backward swing.

In later decades there were many fine acts on the flying trapeze. A triple somersault may have been achieved by Robert Hanlon and the Volta brothers by 1881, though it is not certain whether this was between trapeze and catcher or to the net. A Latvian girl called Lena Jordan was certainly performing one in Australia in 1897, though this was in a casting act, not from a trapeze, and within a year she had grown too big to repeat it. A dozen years later Ernest Clarke was making triples caught by his brother Charles. The brothers were members of an English tenting circus family who had made their first trip to America in 1836 and subsequently travelled all over the world. they formed a team known as the Clarkonians which toured with Lord George Sanger's circus and joined Barnum and Bailey in 1901. There are still Clarke family members performing in American circuses.

Alfredo Codona, son of an English mother and a Mexican father who became known as 'King of the Trapeze,' performed with his father as catcher with the Wirth Circus in Australia in 1913, joining Ringling Brothers in 1917. By then a number of other trapezists had been killed attempting the triple but Codona was determined to include it in his act. After three years of practice he did, at the Chicago Coliseum in 1920, and repeated it many times until the inevitable fall. He is said to have become careless about safety following the death of his second wife, Lillian Leitzel. Though he survived his injuries he could not 'fly' again. (The manner of his death was no less sensational: he shot himself and his third wife in her lawyer's office where they were finalizing their divorce.)

In the 1930s and '40s the Concellos, originally Art(hur) Vas Concello, his wife Antoinette Comeau and their catcher Eddie Ward Junior, were the top flying team. Art, from Spokane, Washington, did not come of circus stock but learned trapeze work as a lad and at 16 joined Ward's family's troupe. Art not only did the triple but could do two backward somersaults with a half twist, a double horizontal pirouette and other feats. From 1933 he began to train other flyers and in 1937 Antoinette made her first triples in public, the first woman to perform them regularly. She took six years out of the ring while she raised their son and when she eventually stopped flying for good she became aerial director for Ringling Brothers. Art moved into management in 1943, but trapeze acts trained and owned by him continued to perform under the name of the Flying Concellos.

The Flying Vazquez, with Miguel Vazquez making his quadruple somersault to catcher Juan Vazquez.

A world record for the consecutive performance of successful triple somersaults was set by the then 18-year-old Jaime Ibarra at Circus World Museum in 1989. A 3.5 somersault was performed in 1962 at Durango in Mexico, by Tony Steel, whose catcher was Lee Manlees. It was later repeated by American acts, the Rock Smith Flyers and the Farfans, whose flyer Don Martinez also achieved it with catcher Basil Schoultz in South Africa. Mexican Tito Gaona of the Flying Gaonas was doing them too – blindfold! An attractive and personable performer and a superb athlete, Gaona was an excellent flyer despite carrying more weight than most.

First to do a triple back somersault with one and a half twists was the glamorous Terry Cavaretta Lemus, at Circus-Circus in Las Vegas, in 1969. She worked with her sister and brother as the Flying Terrels and the Cavarettas were the first act to have all girl flyers.

Circus skills, like those of track and field athletes, are continually being pushed further. Ernest Clarke is said to have made quadruple somersaults in private but never felt confident of performing them publicly. Tito Goana succeeded in doing four backward somersaults, but again only in rehearsal and in fact he was never able to repeat the feat. Miguel Vazquez also did a quadruple in rehearsal and he was eventually able to add it to the Vazquez act in 1982. Though not always successful, he achieved it in 80 per cent of his attempts and set the world record in completed quadruples.

The somersaults and twists executed by a trapeze act are also performed from one platform to another, a type of act said to have been originated by Harry Potter of the Peerless Potters. The flyer is thrown or 'cast' by a thrower or throwers, usually holding them in a hand-to-ankle or wrist-to-wrist grasp and caught by a catcher about 16 feet (4.8 metres) away. The flyer is dependent

MIGUELVAZQUEZ
QUADRUPLE SAUT PÉRILLEUX

HUGO · SIEGRIST · N. RODRIGUEZ

TOP
The Mexican Flying Jimenez, with Raoul Jimenez doing a triple somersault blindfold. They were Circus World Champions until the Koreans introduced a new kind of act incorporating a Russian swing and multiple passes.

ABOVE
The Flying Lantonys, a Columbian-American troupe led by Raul Antionia Lancheros Ruiz with Frank Kora as catcher.

upon the strength of the caster to provide volition. There is usually a wide belt across the platform on which throwers and catchers rest their bodies. Double passes and blindfolds may also be included.

Other apparatus can be used for the catcher instead of a simple trapeze, and in acrobatics similar to trapeze work. Usually known as cradles, these have more horizontal components which an acrobat can stand on or hang from.

Other Aeriel Acts

Ringling Brothers and Barnum and Bailey's aerial ballet on the web.

There are many other spectacular aerial acts in which the performer is suspended. The *corde lisse*, or web, is a simple vertical rope. The performer may use only a twist of the rope around a limb to give support for artistic poses high above the ring or, alternatively, a loop in the rope around a wrist or ankle. Groups of performers on the web can produce effective aerial ballets. A padded loop on a swivel at the end of the rope enables the acrobat to perform vertical swing-overs, or planges, on one arm.

The most famous exponent of these skills was Lillian Leitzel. She was born Lillian Alize Pelikan Eleanore (Leitzel is a diminutive of Alize) in Germany of Czech and Hungarian parents in 1882. Her mother and aunts were in a trapeze act called the Leamy Ladies and it was with that act that she first reached America in 1910.

When they returned to Europe, she stayed on as a solo act. At first she worked only in vaudeville, but she was talent-spotted for the Ringling Brothers in 1915 and within a few years had become one of circus's top stars. As well as working on the single rope, she also performed on the Roman Rings, a pair of rings on ropes like those used by gymnasts but set high above the arena, on which she would perform intricate twists and turns, ending with a handstand. Her temperament was stormy and capricious, and she did not conform easily to Ringling's tight discipline, but she was a favourite of public and circus folk alike. She married the trapeze star Alfredo Codona, in 1927, and they became a quarrelsome but devoted couple. They usually performed on the same bill but in 1931, when they were contemplating retirement from the circus, they accepted separate engagements in Europe. At

the Valencia Music Hall in Copenhagen, she had completed her performance on the Roman Rings and was just starting her multiple planges on the *corde lisse* when the swivel ring supporting her snapped, the metal having been weakened by the constant heating and cooling caused by her turns, and she fell to the ground. Trying to rise she insisted she would continue but was taken to hospital and died there two days later.

More recently, in the 1970s, Fernanda Peris emulated her achievement, turning 160 planges; Leitzel turned 100 at most performances but her record was 249. Dolly Jacobs, daughter of clown Lou Jacobs, has become the contemporary star of the Roman Rings, ending her performance with a somersault from the rings to the web rope for her descent to to the ground.

Instead of hanging by a wrist or ankle some performers hang by their teeth. Such 'iron-jaw' acts may be performed either on the end of a *corde lisse* or from the trapeze. A leather form made from a plaster cast of the mouth, jaw and teeth, fills the entire mouth cavity but allows the teeth to close. This can also be made as a double grip so that someone swinging by their legs or ankles from a trapeze can support another person, spinning mouth to mouth. The three Tybell Sisters, appearing with Adam Forepaugh and Sells Circus in 1910, circled teeth-hanging in the air and flapping costume wings like butterflies to add a variation to this act, an elaboration adopted recently by Bambi Aurora.

If hanging by the teeth seems astounding, what of hanging by the hair? This is an act which has a long history. It used to be a speciality of oriental troupes.

ABOVE
Lillian Leitzel performing on the web, doing her famous multiple planges.

ABOVE RIGHT
Dolly Jacobs on the Roman Rings at the Big Apple Circus.

RIGHT
Judy Murton makes a dental spin on the trapeze.

Barnum and Bailey presented the Ching-Ling-He and Tia Pen Troupes in 1914 in whose acts one head of hair supported up to three acrobats, though it is more usual to support only the owner of the scalp. The acrobat is genuinely supported by the roots of his or her hair, which must be long, thick and strong, one reason why it has been predominantly an act for orientals, though Margarita Vazquez Ayala of the Flying Vazquez family and her daughters are among the leading modern exponents. Juggling, which is naturally more difficult when the body is spinning (and spin it must when hanging from a single point), is a more frequent feature of such acts than acrobatics.

To prepare for the act, the wetted hair is divided into sections as it hangs forward and each section braided, incorporating a longer length of strong cord or wire. Each braid is pulled through a relatively small metal ring, wrapped around itself and, if it is long enough, taken through the ring again. The cord ends are then tied firmly to the ring. A hook on the support cable can be slipped through the ring to give suspension and haul the performer up into the air.

This fixing cannot be entirely guaranteed. Ayala, who performed as Marguerite Michelle, fell at Ringling's in 1982 when one of the cords through her hair broke. She was in a coma for three weeks and was unable to return to the act until 1985. However, she taught her act to her daughters Michelle and Andrea and in 1990-91 they performed together, though now they appear as individual artists. All present the same act: as they rise into the air they shed the jump suit they are wearing and begin to spin hoops on their legs while simultaneously spinning three plates on sticks held in the hands and mouth. They are then lowered to the ground to change their apparatus and rise again with more hoops, which they spin on the legs and on the arms. Three hoops are spun on each arm, two going in one direction, one in the other. Lowered to change props again, they juggle flaming torches, ending the act by whirling around in spinning pirouettes.

The cloud swing is a loop of rope used like a trapeze, known much earlier as the *corde volante*. It has made a comeback in recent years, especially with flamboyant performers in the open air such as Englishman Graham Blandini, who has appeared at gala shows in Canada and Australia. Another exponent, Franco di Angelo, appeared at the Blackpool Tower Circus in the 1980s, and numerous 'New Circus' performers have worked on the cloud swing.

In contrast, a recent innovation with no precedent has been the introduction into circus of the elasticated rope used for bungee jumps. This has been taken up by the Chinese and by some of the 'New Circus' troupes, who have exploited the technique to create graceful and spectacular acts.

A poster of 1914 promoting two Chinese troupes performing hair hangs, plate-spinning and other acts. Note the acrobats top left and right travelling on a pulley rather than suspended on a rope.

THE BARN

P.T. BARNUM   J.A. BAILEY

FIRST TIME IN AMERICA OF THE
IMPERIAL CHINESE CIRCUS STARS

Clowns

Comedy has been part of circus from the very beginning, originally in the form of comic horsemanship: the inept tailor and country bumpkin acts were often performed by the same riders who demonstrated the highest skills. The concept of the circus clown is closely linked with the traditions of the Italian *Commedia dell'Arte* and the pantomime Harlequinade, but all subsequent clowns look back to Joseph Grimaldi, the great English actor-clown of the early 19th century, whose father was involved with Hughes's Royal Circus in London. As a little boy Grimaldi appeared as a monkey on a chain in his father's act, but his father died when he was ten and young Joey's career was always in theatres, especially Sadler's Wells. Elements of his costume and make-up (he was one of, if not the first to paint geometric patterns on his face), and some of his material were copied by Andrew Ducrow and by circus clowns.

Clowning was at first one of the all-round skills of circus performers, combined with tumbling and riding, and clowning has been applied to almost all kinds of circus act either as part of a featured act or as a parody of it, performed while the next act is set up. The clowns were also the ring assistants, holding the balloons and ribbons for the riders to leap through and over, engaging in a little repartee to give the acrobat a breathing space or time to prepare their apparatus.

Much of the comedy of the clowns was verbal and directed to the audience. For a time there was a vogue for 'Shakespearean' clowns: Charles Marsh claimed to be the first, though W. F. Wallet became the best known. They seem to have performed a pastiche of speeches from Shakespeare, the originals of which audiences could easily recognize.

In America Wallet worked for a time in partnership with clown and sometime circus proprietor Dan Rice. Rice, born Daniel McLaren, started in circus as a strongman and later had a 'talking' pig called Lord Byron. He had also been a jockey (until he became too heavy) and a card-sharper on the river boats. He sang comic songs of his own composition, often lampooning topical events and people, caught cannon balls on the back of his neck and kept up a lively repartee with the audience. His costume and appearance were very individual. His piercing eyes were set in a long face accentuated by chin whiskers which jutted forward, and he wore a red and white striped tunic and breeches, continued in one stocking only, and an incongruous top hat. It has sometimes been suggested that his appearance was caricatured by Thomas Nast in his symbolic Uncle Sam. Rice was a generous man to others; he often performed for charity and laid on special performances for orphanages. In the era of the Civil War, he was an outspoken unionist (he performed before Abraham Lincoln), which displeased many spectators and contributed to the failure of his company. After the war he formed a successful new circus, but in 1866 decided to go

RIGHT
A clown advertising a British touring company,
Rosaire's Big Circus.

BELOW
A Calvert Litho Company clown poster available for use by
any circus. Costume and make-up show close links to those
used by Joseph Grimaldi at Sadler's Wells in London.

BELOW RIGHT
French clown Jean-Baptiste Auriol dancing on bottles.
As well as being funny he was an acrobat and a leaper who
would jump over 24 soldiers with fixed bayonets or over 12
men on horseback.

into politics. He was not a successful politician and soon returned to the circus, buying a portable amphitheatre from Spalding with borrowed money. Economic recession ruined him and he turned to drink. Later, supposedly having given up the bottle, he stumped the country giving temperance lectures. Further attempts to return to circus failed and he died penniless, a fate all too common among circus artists.

When American circuses developed into huge three-ring spectaculars, they left no place for verbal comedy and that style of individual clown disappeared. In the big arenas clowns more usually appeared en masse, the anarchic chaos of their antics – in fact, of course, based on precise drill – heightening by contrast the disciplined skills of other artists. These clowns would enter, sometimes dozens at a time, working their way around the track and performing their particular speciality for successive sections of the audience.

In Europe individual clowns retained their prominence, though frequently working in pairs, typically the white-face and the *auguste* (German slang for 'clumsy fool'), and sometimes in large groups. The white-face, tending to be severe and domineering, became more florid as the 19th century neared its end, with a costume less suited to tumbling and knock-about. The 'clumsy fool' had always been around but the more grotesque form of the *auguste* is usually said to have been invented by 25-year-old Tom Belling, son of an American circus director, in 1869, when he was with the Circus Renz in Berlin. Claims have also been made for both James Guyon and another English clown called Chadwick, who worked in Paris. Belling's own account is that he was fooling around wearing a big coat inside-out and a wig back to front when Renz saw him and sent him into the ring, where he promptly fell on his face to laughter and shouts of 'Auguste!'. A great variety of grotesque *augustes* have been created since, but Tom, Robert and Clement Belling were still doing their father's act in the 1920s.

One prominent European clown was a Spaniard, Jerome Medrano. Born in 1849, he was apprenticed to a trapezist and jumper called Ballageur and made his debut on the flying trapeze. But he preferred clowning and became Boum Boum, working at the Cirque Fernando and, with a black clown known as Chocolat, at the Nouveau Cirque in Paris. He later mounted a trapeze act at the Hippodrome, and in 1897 he became proprietor of Fernando Beert's circus which, after his death in 1910, continued to operate as the Medrano until 1963.

Chocolat, who gave his name as Padila in his will although even his wife called herself Madame Chocolat, was vague about his origins but claimed to come from Cuba. In Paris in 1889 he paired up with an English clown called Footit, who came from a circus family and had been an accomplished rider and acrobat at the age of 12. It is said that he turned to clowning after he lost his horse in a poker game. Before going to Paris he had toured Britain as Funny Footit in an act with a performing hippopotamus. Together, Footit and Chocolat became a great attraction at the Nouveau Cirque: Footit in white-face, the taller Chocolat the much put-upon *auguste*. The inherent racism of society was reflected in the indignities inflicted by the haughty clown on his good-natured black partner but, to be fair, this was essentially the role of all *augustes* and Chocolat received equal billing with Footit, a situation not to be found in the United States, where the circus largely relegated blacks to the role of roustabouts, or minor members of the clown troupe.

The world of the Paris circus was memorably portrayed by Henri de Toulouse-Lautrec, and Footitt was a favourite subject, easily recognized by the tuft of hair at the front of his head, while Chocolat appears dancing, rather elegantly in fact, in a bar. The ring at the Nouveau Cirque could be lowered and flooded, and this facility was employed for 'Chocolat's Wedding', an act involving a stolen pig in which the bride was carried off

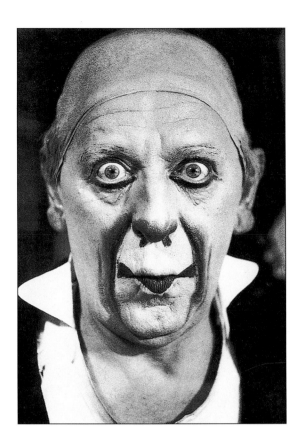

OPPOSITE ABOVE
Footit and Chocolat at the Nouveau Cirque, drawn by Henri de Toulouse-Lautrec for the single issue of his satirical magazine Nib, *issued with the* Révue Blanche.

OPPOSITE BELOW
Chocolat dancing in a bar, drawn by Henri de Toulouse-Lautrec for Le Rire *in 1896.*

LEFT
Grock, the musical clown who could play 17 different instruments.

RIGHT
Anatoli Marchevsky, clown star of the Moscow State Circus, noted for his 'flower power' clothes and lack of traditional make-up. To end one show he mimed cutting open his chest and giving the audience his heart to thank them for their warmth and applause.

BELOW
Oleg Popov, famous Russian clown. In 1981 he was presented with a Gold Clown award by Princess Grace (former film star Grace Kelly) at the Monte Carlo Circus Festival.

by students and the wedding party ended up being thrown into the water.

Later *entrée* clowns have more usually worked in threes. In a typical scenario one plays some kind of trick upon the second but is observed by the third who then enters forewarned and when it is tried on him is able to turn the trick against its originator. Some routines, often adapted from centuries-old prototypes, are perennially revived. And not always in new form: the Fratellinis had a barber-shop routine which the Busch circus tried to ban because it had been seen so often before, but the clowns ignored instructions and still brought the house down!

The Fratellinis were brothers whose father had become a gymnast and acrobatic clown after meeting circus folk when fighting with Garibaldi's nationalists in Italy. François became an acrobatic rider, the others tumbling clowns. All worked together for a time but later they split up. François, with one brother Paul and Paul's wife, a rider, formed an equestrian act, while the others opted for burlesque acrobatics. After the death of another brother, Louis, in 1909, François sold his horses and they began to work together again as clowns, taking joint responsibility for Louis's three children. François became the white-face, Paul a rotund drole and Albert the *auguste*; all were also musicians. In one routine typical of their acts François, in a spangled coat, has a little repartee with the ringmaster before the pompous figure of Paul enters in a big black coat and top hat. They agree to a little chamber music, François on mandolin, Paul on guitar, and after some deliberation they settle on chairs in the middle of the ring playing a lively tune on the mandolin with solemn, meditative twangs from the guitar. Then, in a sort of jerky, prowling gait, in comes the red-nosed, grotesquely bewigged Albert in a vast, trailing coat, enormous shoes and trousers that keep falling down, carrying a huge bass tuba. He interrupts them with an ear-shattering blast. Shocked, they stop, look round indignantly, but Albert has disappeared. After much byplay, they find him, silence his intrusive tuba by stuffing his coat down its horn, and exit playing harmoniously together.

The Fratellinis' children continued the tradition. Paul's son Victor developed a Chaplinesque trapeze act, François's sons Kiko, Henri (Popol) and François (Baba) were comedy acrobats reviving some of the family acts, and Victor's daughter Annie, after a successful career as dancer, instrumentalist and singer, returned to circus as a clown and set up her own circus school in Paris. Tino, son of Baba, was an outstanding comedy acrobat with Circus Roncalli until his premature death at 47 in 1994. With his partner, Toni, he performed a delightful parody of an old-time comedy acrobatic act.

The Rastellis were also among the top European musical clowns. Members of the same family as the famous juggler, they were led for many decades by Oreste Rastelli and, after his death in 1962, by his son Alfredo, who paired with grandson Orestino as twin *augustes* and was joined by two Brazilians: Antonio Poletto and Aristedes Ferreira, both accomplished on the trampoline.

The spangled coat that has become traditional for the continental white-face clown was probably introduced by Antonet, a one time partner of Grock. Today's most elegant white-face clowns are Francesco Caroli with

BELOW LEFT
Coco the Clown, associated for many years with the Bertram Mills Circus, was awarded the O.B.E. by Queen Elizabeth II.

He worked until aged 74 and died in 1959.

A rather different type of clown was the Italian Enrico Sprocani, working as Rhum, who in 1924, aged 20, appeared in an *entrée* based on the death of Hamlet in the Cirque Royale in Brussels. He was very much an actor rather than a knock-about clown, and his act was full of pathos and subtleties. Others were to explore this aspect later.

The Russian clown Oleg Popov, internationally famous with the Moscow State Circus, certainly thought of himself more as a comedian than a clown and sought to avoid grotesquerie and knock-about. He worked as a compositor for the newspaper Pravda and was an amateur acrobat and entertainer until he got his chance in circus standing in for a clown friend who was ill. Only after that, aged 20, did he go to Moscow's circus school. One of his mentors was Karandash, who pioneered the Russian style that avoids absurd costume and heavy make-up.

ABOVE
Emmett Kelly, the great American clown.

Roncalli, Alexis Gruss with his own circus and Pipo Sosman with the Arlette Gruss Circus.

The famous Grock, whose real name was Adrian Wettach, was another musical clown. He could play 17 instruments, and was also an acrobat who could juggle on the tightrope. He entered the ring, a diminutive figure, weighed down by an enormous cabin trunk, which he carried round and round the ring until at last he found a place to put it down. Then, from its huge bulk he would extract the tiniest of violins and begin to play.

Grock was the son of a Geneva watchmaker, who worked as a gymnast at weekend fairs and festivals. When only seven Adrian ran off to join the tenting circus of a Spanish clown family, the Barracetas, who did an act combining musicianship and comic songs with high-wire juggling and acrobatics. In his mid teens he left the circus and worked as a waiter, piano tuner and French teacher, but in 1910, when he was 30, he returned to circus with a quartet of musicians he had formed. He and Antonet modified their style to work in theatres and he could sustain his act for an hour or more, though never allowed that long in the ring. He ran his own non-animal circus and had a number of other partners, including Hans Brick (better known as an animal trainer), with whom he did acrobatic and balletic acts in variety theatres, where Grock attracted very high fees.

Karandash based his humour on natural behaviour, not caricature. The not-too-bright character he impersonated attempted to emulate the skills of other performers and, on the slack wire and as a juggler, he could match some of the best. In fact, in many ways his style was a return to the clowning of the early circus.

One of Charlie Chaplin's first jobs as a boy was with the then well-known clown Marceline in pantomime at the London Hippodrome. He was supposed to be a cat drinking a bowl of milk whom the clown falls over as he backs away from a dog, and earns a reprimand for not arching his back correctly to break the clown's fall. Marceline (real name Isadore Orbes) worked with a small poodle trained to copy his every action. He was successful in America until fashions changed, and he became a night-club impresario. He lost all his money and shot himself.

Chaplin never appeared in circus, except on film, but other clowns have paid tribute to him by reproducing his 'little man', and his character influenced the development of the hobo clown. However, several other big cinema names did start in circus, among them Harry Langdon, a white-face before he went to Hollywood, Red Skelton, who ran away from home to join the Hagenbeck-Wallace Circus, and Burt Lancaster, a circus acrobat, as well as W. C. Fields and Eddie Cantor. For the great

Buster Keaton, the pattern was reversed. After his silent film career came to an end he appeared in the ring at the Cirque Medrano.

Charlie Rivel, leading member of the Rivels trio who were of old Spanish circus stock, developed an imitation of the Chaplin 'little man' on the trapeze which was probably the best. This was only one of many manifestations of his talent, which included a burlesque of a *prima donna* in a long red shift and a variety of instrumental turns.

Another Charlie, Charlie Cairoli, trained by his father at the Medrano in Paris and a permanent fixture at Blackpool Tower Circus in England from 1939 to 1979, presented a little man in business suit and bowler hat. Cairoli was a versatile musical clown, as good at subtleties as slapstick. For 40 years he entertained generations of youngsters as parents and grandparents returned with their children and grandchildren to enjoy again the clowning that had delighted them when they were young.

Latvian-born Coco, with his wig sticking out in all directions and his zany *auguste*'s clothes, was another British favourite, especially with children. He became a household name in Britain while he was with the Bertram Mills Circus, in 1929-67. His son Michael is now famous as Coco in the United States. The original Coco was crippled in a road accident in 1959 but returned to the ring and, after retiring when Bertram Mills closed, made a comeback with the Robert Brothers Circus in 1974, shortly before he died. Coco's publicity work for road safety earned him the OBE (Order of the British Empire) in 1963.

America too has had its clown stars. At the beginning of this century Frank 'Slivers' Oakley, whose parents were Swedish, became especially famous for the act in which he mimed each member of a baseball team, for which he was given a five-minute solo spot at Madison Square Garden. He left Ringling in 1907 and in the following years became increasingly eccentric and less appealing. In 1916 he went to Otto Ringling to ask for his old job back but was offered only walk-about clowning at $50 instead of the $750 he had earned before. A few days later he committed suicide.

Felix Adler from Clinton, Iowa, with his tiny umbrella and nose that lit up when he got excited, was famous a little later. He performed so often before presidents that he became known as the White House clown. His 'signature' act involved a little pig, and as each pig grew too large he had to train another one to climb steps and scoot down a slide board. In five decades he is said to have trained more than 500 pigs!

Otto Griebling emigrated from Germany when he was 15 and first worked in America as a bareback rider. Ten years later he tried his hand at clowning, creating a sad tramp character who was an instant success. He was one of several hobo clowns inspired by the Depression of the 1930s and was influenced by Chaplin. In one typical routine he carried around a block of ice, trying to find someone who would accept delivery. He failed to get any takers but refused to give up, though the ice melted, growing smaller and smaller until it disappeared altogether. The well-known act in which a great number of clowns emerge from a tiny car was said to be his invention. The Studebaker company told him it was impossible to make a car that could hold 26 people, but he devised a way. To cap the effect, the last occupant to emerge carried an enormous prop.

Lou Jacobs, another German immigrant, began as a

Peter Shub, American comic mime with the European Roncalli Circus, came to prominence when he won a prize at the Cirque de Demain (Circus of Tomorrow) in Paris in 1986. As an American tourist complete with tripod and tiny camera, and in his other routines, he scores superbly with the audience by being one of them and by having the nerve to ask them to do things with him which, in the highly charged atmosphere of Circus Roncalli, they invariably do.

Lou Jacobs with his dog Knucklehead disguised as a rabbit for his famous hunting gag.

contortionist-clown. He arrived in the United States in 1923 and within two years had been engaged by Ringling. He is probably best remembered for his motorized contrivances and especially his entrance in a minuscule car, backfiring and spluttering, from which eventually his huge bulk emerged, enlarged by a vast coat and enormous boots. Equally famous was his hunting sketch in which his little dog, with the addition of a pair of elongated ears, impersonated a rabbit. His clown face was used worldwide on posters as a symbol of the circus and in 1966 appeared on a U.S. postage stamp.

Emmett Kelly came from Sedan, Kansas. He was famous as 'Weary Willie,' a character he first invented in 1920 as a cartoon for the film company where he was an artist. He sold tickets, painted stands and performed as a trapezist and sometimes a white-face clown but, though he often thought of introducing his hobo character to the ring, such an innovation was resisted. It was not until 1932 that Willie was finally accepted by the circus.

The American clown developed a markedly different character from his counterpart in Europe. They generally worked in larger numbers, wore more colourful clothes and more exaggerated make-up, but on both sides of the Atlantic the individual clown developed his (or occasionally her) own appearance and make-up, and it was understood throughout the profession that, however much they might have been influenced by predecessors, every clown's make-up was his personal property, not to be worn by anyone else.

Modern clowns have often abandoned the grotesque for a more natural character. Jean-Paul, for instance, who has appeared with Circus Knie and Roncalli, wears no make-up at all but wanders around the ring as the audience comes in and gets himself hired by the ringmaster. Others have used white-face in its most classic *commedia* style. There is a place for all, from the most hilarious slapstick to the most sentimental pathos. There is a place for both the individual, such as the Russian Slava Polunin, currently stunning audiences world-wide with his Snow Show, or Big Apple's Grandma (Barry Lubin), and for the often repeated *entrées* for groups of clowns such as the house on fire, when a squad of comic firemen rush around in the fire wagon to rescue people, or man the reversed sausage machine that churns out a trained dog.

A recent trend in circus comedy has been to allow a star clown to involve members of the audience in the routine, as when David Shiner, with Knie, invites an attractive young woman to join him and mimes taking her out for a date in his 'sports car', improvised from two chairs. Inevitably the car breaks down and together they have plenty of adventures which follow a basic plot but depend for their success upon the spectator willingly indulging the spirit of fantasy. As the imagination of the whole audience is drawn into participating in a unique performance the effect can be magical. This style of audience participation has worked superbly in one-ring circuses, as with Shiner, or Peter Shub of Roncalli or René Bazinet with Cirque du Soleil, but many were surprised when Ringling producer Kenneth Feld booked Italian clown David Larible for his vast three-ring circus in 1991. The success of this reinstatement of the importance of the solo clown is evidenced by Larible's starring presence with Ringling ever since. He brings the classic manner up to date, interacting with the ringmaster, going high into the tiered seating to bring out volunteers for a comic love scene and, as his sister Vivian does her solo trapeze act, serenading her on the trumpet.

Animal Acts

Without the horse there would have been no circus, but other animals were present from the start as well. There were monkeys rope-walking or riding, dogs doing tricks, as well as 'learned' animals, particularly pigs. Dancing bears had been seen at markets in the Middle Ages; a Renaissance parade featured a 'cat organ', made up of cats selected for the pitch of their miaow. Numerous street acts featured doves and other birds. Grimaldi had ducks pulling a cart, another clown preferred pigs for the task, and a clown called Dickie Usher harnessed cats (though it has been suggested that the cat carts were actually pedalled). All kinds of exotic creatures were exhibited alone or in menageries in Britain and continental Europe and later in America too, while in the ring Ducrow was already exhibiting a team of trained zebras in 1832.

The more unusual or dangerous the animal the bigger the attraction, and keepers in the 19th century introduced an element of performance to what had been merely an exhibition by entering the cages of lions and tigers in public view – and not underplaying the danger of the exploit. At Atkins's Menagerie in 1829 the British could see a lion and a tigress jump through a hoop and their keeper put his head inside the lion's mouth. In

Gunther Gebel-Williams and one of his tigers riding an elephant, a major star with Ringling Brothers and Barnum and Bailey until his retirement in 1990.

France Henri Martin was staging fights with his big cats and hyenas. He brought them to London in 1832, appearing with them in a play at Drury Lane and the following year both he and Winney, Atkins's trainer, showed their animals at Astley's. Winney was able to introduce a litter of playful hybrid cubs to the audience.

In America the following year a trainer called Ray appeared with Raymond and Ogden's Menagerie and a Mr Roberts, billed as 'from London', with the National Menagerie. That autumn Roberts was mauled by a tiger while touring Connecticut and this gave a 22-year-old cage attendant, Isaac Van Amburgh, a chance to take his place. Van Amburgh, a Dutch-American with a Native American grandfather, had an amazing rapport with his animals, engaging in friendly play with them, which he was soon demonstrating at the Richmond Hill Theatre, New York. He became the most famous of animal trainers, plays being specially written to feature him and his animals. He went to London in 1838 and had a sensational success at both Astley's and Drury Lane Theatre, performing before the young Queen Victoria and then touring the country as partner in a combined circus and menagerie. He appeared in gladiator costume and his act included a lion lying down with a lamb. Edwin

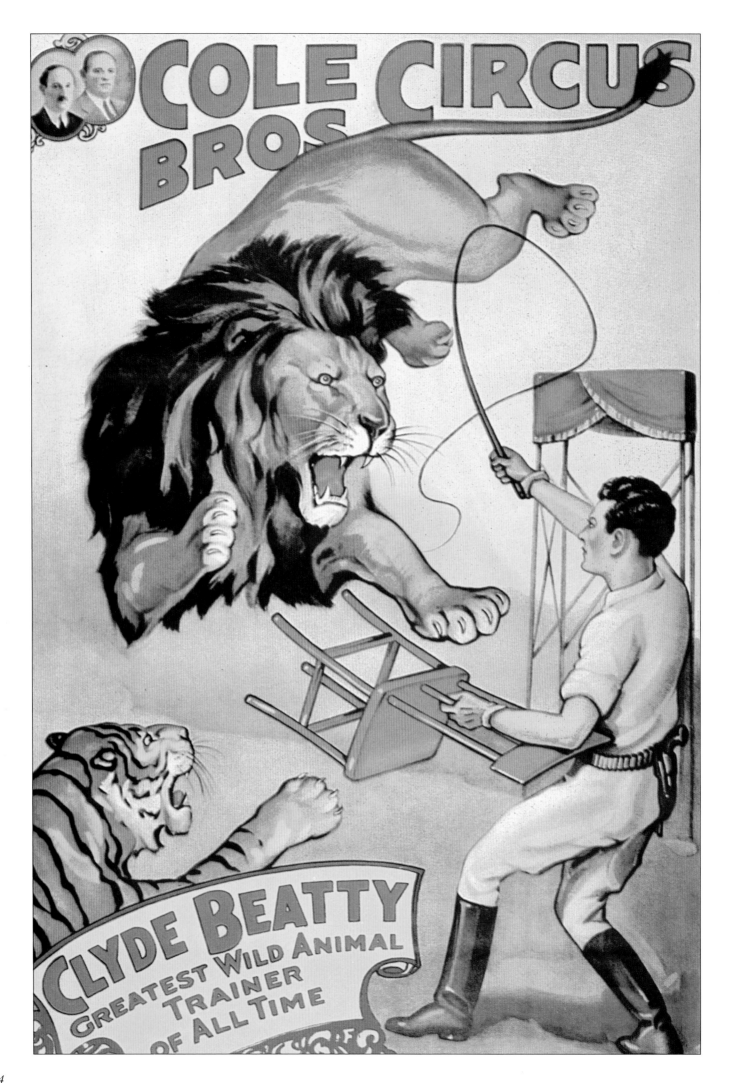

OPPOSITE
Clyde Beatty, American animal trainer and best known exponent of the fighting style of wild-animal act.

LEFT
Mabel Stark, foremost American woman animal trainer of her time, with Prince, one of her Bengal tigers. She was still presenting big cats in the ring in her seventies.

BELOW
Mabel Stark with tigers and her black jaguar in the early days of her career.

Landseer painted him and he became a popular subject for Staffordshire pottery. A correspondent of the *Nairnshire Telegraph* saw his performance in Scotland:

'After a demonstration of the giraffe, Van Amburgh, dressed as Rollo, with a whip in hand, dashed through the back door into one of the cages of which a lioness, a tiger and three beautiful leopards were the occupants. He was saluted by a savage growl from the tiger, who stood erect on his hind legs against the bars of the cage, while the lion maintained a dignified appearance and the leopards continued to gambol around the den. Van Amburgh appeared to be in his element among those dread rulers of their native forests, whom he sometimes hugged, teased, cuffed and pushed about. Leaving the den, he entered another with whose rough inmates he used the same familiarity and actually put his face into a lion's mouth; during all of which the spectators could scarce repress a shudder of horror.'

Back in the United States Van Amburgh toured with his own menagerie and circus, which continued to bear his name many years after his death.

Many others followed, among them the American Lion King, John Carter, who was at Astley's in 1839 and stayed in Britain for some years. In the next decade women trainers were appearing. Ellen Chapman, presented by Wombwell's Menagerie as Pauline de Vere, was the first woman to put her head into a lion's mouth; she too became a popular Staffordshire figure. Other famous animal trainers of the mid-19th century included a Zulu called Maccomo, who worked in both America and England, and James Crockett, who starred in George Sanger's Circus in 1857 and had a great success in Europe with another Englishman named Lucas .

In America Jacob Driesbach became celebrated as the century progressed. He may have been the first who,

Suzanne Chipperfield, descendant of a long line of performers and animal trainers, presenting one of her tigers in Peter Jay's Superdome Circus, on Blackpool Pleasure Beach, opened when the owners of the Tower Circus no longer permitted showing animals there.

realizing that people were excited most by the risk to the trainer, decided to exploit the natural ferocity of the animals. He trained a leopard to spring at him as he was working with the lion. People flocked to experience this thrill, and some of them fainted in horror when they saw him apparently attacked from both sides.

In America especially it became the usual form in wild animal acts to emphasize their ferocious power in attack (*en ferocité*). In Europe emphasis was placed on the skill of the trainer in controlling the animals (*en pelotage*). This more restrained performance is said to be actually more dangerous. In recent years it has become more common in American circuses too.

Two of the biggest American names of the early 20th century, Mabel Stark and Clyde Beatty, were taught

Josip Marcan, embraced by his white tiger in the ring at the Enis Togni Circus.

their skills by the Hungarian trainer Louis Roth when they joined circuses where he was employed. Mabel Stark, Toronto-born though raised in Kentucky, was training as a nurse when she had a breakdown. Recuperating in California, she saw a stunt man wrestle a tiger. Fascinated, she bought the tiger and tried to train it, and in 1912, aged 20, took a job as stable girl with the Al G. Barnes Circus. She graduated to circus rider and Barnes coaxed a reluctant Louis Roth into teaching her his knowledge of animal training. Within a few years the pupil had become the star, wrestling tigers in a white

Poster promoting Togare, famous wild animal trainer with this great British circus during the 1930s and immediately after the Second World War.

leather suit and using neither whip, pistol nor even a chair as protection. One tiger, Rajah, was 350 lb (159 kg), huge compared to the petite Stark, but she would roll him over and put her face in his mouth. She had three years with Ringling Brothers, until they briefly abandoned big-cat acts in 1925, and did not retire from the ring until four months before her death in 1967.

At the age of seven Clyde Beatty of Bainbridge, Ohio, was already teaching tricks to his domestic pets and putting on a show. In 1918, then 16, he joined Howes's Great London Circus (an American show

despite the name) as cage boy, where he too learned from trainer Louis Roth. Two years later he was presenting an act with six bears. He was with the Hagenback-Wallace Circus when their trainer had a heart attack and was given his chance with big cats. He went on to develop a very personal style which for years represented the popular image of a lion tamer. Dressed like Hollywood's idea of an African white hunter, he wielded a metal-reinforced chair, a revolver which fired blanks and a whip, used only to crack to get attention. In 1934 he formed his own circus with the Cole Brothers. His

dramatic performances with gun shots and snarling beasts continued until his death from cancer in 1965.

The Frenchman Alfred Court, who became the leading exponent of the European school, had his own Zoo Circus in France between the world wars. He had been a circus acrobat since he was 15 but was 35 before he set foot in a lion's cage in 1917. At that time he was director of a small circus on tour in Mexico and, as he told the story, the lion cage had already been set up ready for the second half of a show and the audience was already returning to its seats when the lion tamer was found dead drunk. Court had to fill the breach. He noticed a pile of raw meat ready to feed the big cats after their performance and decided to feed them in the ring. The ring boy warned him that they were always fed singly so that they did not fight over their food, but Court had the meat wheeled into the ring anyway and announced, *'Our tamer has been detained at the frontier ... The lion's performance cannot be given until tomorrow ... Nevertheless you are about to witness a sensational spectacle which has never before been exhibited – feeding the lions!'*

As he left the ring the band played and the lions were let in. Each in turn saw the meat and took a chunk off into a corner, then two began to quarrel over a leg and the fight escalated. When the meat was gone it took 15 minutes and round after round of (blank) pistol shots to clear the ring but, after their initial disappointment, the audience loved it. No replacement trainer could be found so the drunk had to be reinstated but Court watched him – and hence his act – carefully, it had a dramatic finale in which the biggest lion was forced against the bars, the trainer retreated as the lion bounded after him and interposed a chair which the lion tore to pieces until the trainer fired a pistol, the signal for the lion to run down the tunnel out of the ring. At a rehearsal, Court was invited into the cage and, equipped with his own protective chair, found himself drawn into the act. A few days later the trainer was drunk again and Court decided to attempt the act on his own. Putting on the trainer's costume he tried a rehearsal and found that the lions

Gunther Gebel-Williams with leopards and black panthers in the ring with Ringling Brothers and Barnum and Bailey Circus.

RIGHT
Wjatislaw Zolkin's Russian bears take part in a foot-juggling act at Monte Carlo.

remembered their routine much better than he did. Thus he became a presenter of lions! And not only lions: he later presented no less than 18 animals of six different species in the ring and called his act *'Peace in the Jungle'*. He went to Ringling in 1940 with three such wild-animal acts, which were presented simultaneously in the three rings by his protégés.

Court, undoubtedly a great trainer, followed the methods for training wild animals that were developed by Karl Hagenbeck. Karl's father, Gottfried Hagenbeck (or Hägenbach, as it is more correctly spelled), was a fishmonger in Hamburg who acquired a group of seals accidentally caught in fishing nets. This and young Karl's enthusiasm for animals led them to become one of the world's biggest animals dealers, supplying menageries, zoos and circuses. The family started their own circus in 1887, which became internationally renowned and survived until financial problems put it out of business in 1953.

In 1903, Karl also established a zoo, at Stellingen, a suburb of Hamburg, which revolutionized ways of keeping captive animals by putting them in landscaped compounds rather than in cages. However, it was in animal training and exhibiting that Karl had the biggest influence. In 1888 he introduced the circular ring cage for showing animals, which previously had been seen in the ring in their ordinary cages. This greatly facilitated performances *en pelotage*, allowing the animals to display their beauty and agility. One of his trainers, Julius Seeth, around 1900 was showing 21 lions presented to Hagenbeck by the Emperor of Ethiopia. He wore the gold-braided military uniform that was much copied by others working with big cats. Hagenbeck was a lover of animals and was disgusted by the displays of brute force he saw in some circuses, both in the ring and in training. He adopted a gentler approach (employed by Henri Martin half a century before). His method was based on rewards for 'correct' behaviour and no reward, or a mild rebuke, for 'wrong' behaviour. He believed in starting the training young and rejected any animals whose temperament seemed unsuitable.

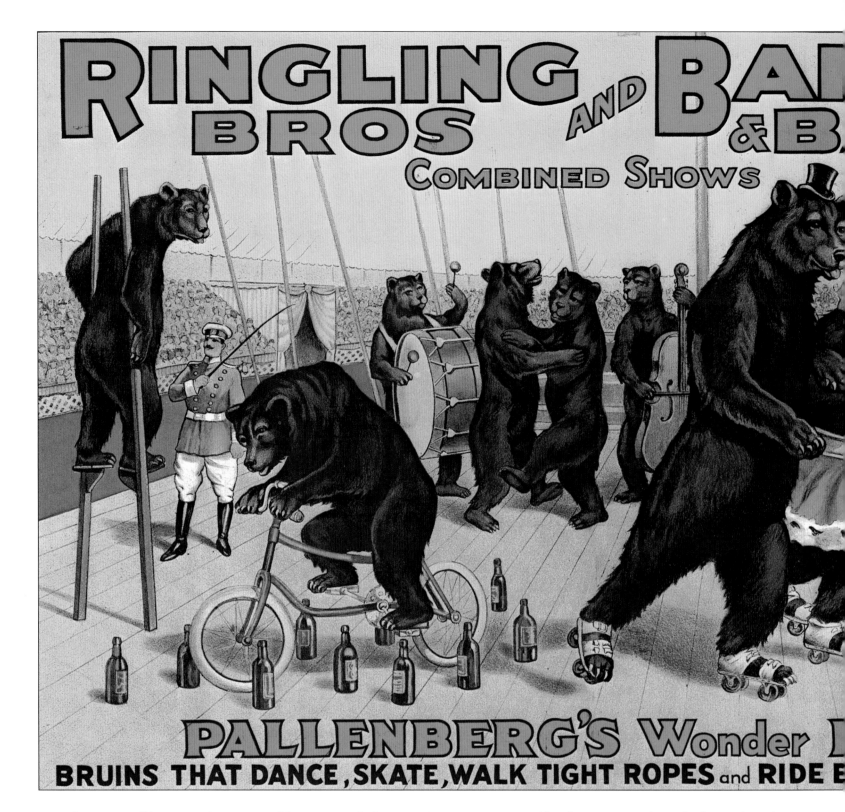

RINGLING BROS AND BA... &B... COMBINED SHOWS

PALLENBERG'S Wonder ...
BRUINS THAT DANCE, SKATE, WALK TIGHT ROPES and RIDE ...

'Pallenberg's Wonder Bears' in a poster of the 1920s.

As any responsible pet owner knows, successful training of animals utilizes and reinforces aspects of their natural behaviour. The same is true of performing animals, though sometimes an action may occur by accident and the animals can be encouraged to repeat it. Actions must match the animal's physique: it is, for instance, much more difficult for a tall animal to maintain a difficult balance.

The trust an animal develops in its trainer overcomes its natural defensive or aggressive instincts in interaction with that trainer, and perhaps other people. But what of creatures who in nature represent predator and prey? How, for instance, is a herbivore to be trained to accept its natural predator leaping upon its back, or the predator to refrain from killing it?

It helps if animals are reared away from the wild, and modern circus animals have been captive-bred for generations. Living in sight and smell of another creature

without harm, a creature that carries the same keeper's scent, or even its own scent transferred by mutual contact with the trainer, encourages familiarity and perhaps blurs identification as 'danger' or 'dinner'. But it needs more than that for a horse to allow a tiger on its back! As well as acclimatizing the animal so that it does not take instant flight, the horse will first be accustomed to having a small animal, such as a dog, jump on to it, while the tiger is taught first to leap from pedestal to pedestal, then on to a moving target, until the leap has become an action in itself, not a stage in killing prey. Mary Chipperfield of the British circus family, a trainer of animals for other circuses and filmwork as well as being a famous equestrienne and animal presenter, uses just such methods. Her cousin Dicky Chipperfield Junior trained the leopards and panthers in his act to leap on to his back as they jumped between pedestals around the ring and to lie on top of him on the ground, suppressing all natural instinct

RNUM
AILEY

EARS
CYCLES LIKE HUMANS

when, during a performance with the Chipperfields' Circus, the lights suddenly failed and he found himself being squeezed by a large female. To his relief he realized the bear was shivering in fright and had clung to him for safety and reassurance, a touching example of the rapport that develops between animals and their trainers. But it is also worth remembering that one trainer, Jack Hubert, lost both his arms in separate incidents, one to a lion and the other to a bear.

The most famous bear trainers were the Pallenbergs, from Germany. Emil and his wife Catherine moved to the United States in 1914 to join Ringling Brothers and showed huge Russian bears which danced, roller-skated, bicycled, played musical instruments and walked the tightrope. Many of the tricks they introduced became standard in bear acts. Louis Roth and Clyde Beatty both trained bears, Beatty starting with a polar-bear act before he went on to big cats. A backward somersault in his act was developed when a standing bear clutched him during rehearsal. When Beatty punched it on the nose it spun over backwards, and a tap on the face became the cue to perform the turn. He also taught bears to march in a circle and to ride bicycles. Albert Rix, an ex-Hagenbeck trainer who first appeared with Ringling in the early 1950s, developed breeding groups of various types of bear in the United States. Not surprisingly, Russian circuses have developed some fine acts with Russian bears. The Kaseevs' bear troupe used to dance the *pas de quatre* from Swan Lake.

HARVARD COLLEGE LIBRARY, THEATRE COLLECTION

to attack the trainer in this vulnerable position. Such trust was evident in some of the earliest acts and has been seen in the performances of Gunther Gebel-Williams, whose leopards performed similar feats. The Chipperfields and James Clubb in Britain, and John Cuneo's Hawthorn Organization in the United States, can train animal groups and pass them on to others to present, but changes of handler must be very carefully planned. The animals need to get thoroughly accustomed to the new handler, for this is a more intimate matter than simply adopting exactly the same cues for the routine as those with which the animals have become familiar.

All such acts still involve a considerable element of risk and not only with the big cats. Bears, which have been trained for many hundreds of years, may seem big cuddly creatures, but a powerful brown bear can be very dangerous. One of James Clubb's own acts involved bears and he thought, momentarily, that he was at serious risk

Jumbo, the famous elephant from London Zoo, which Barnum made a phenomenal attraction in America.

Polar bears were one of the first exotics to be exhibited in America: a Greenland bear was shown in Boston in 1733. But they became comparatively more rare in circuses because they require such carefully managed living conditions. However, the East German troupe of Ursula Bottcher was successful with polar bears at Ringling Brothers in the 1970s.

Performing elephants were for many years one of the most popular acts in circus. In 1941, they even had a ballet specially commissioned. Ringling Brothers persuaded Igor Stravinsky and Georges Balanchine to create the music and choreography for the Circus Polka, featuring their elephant Modoc. Elephants have been trained as working animals for centuries in India and were used in battle by Indian rulers and by the Carthaginians, but a trained elephant did not appear as a circus act until 1812, when Baba danced a few steps, waved a handkerchief and presented a lady in the audience with

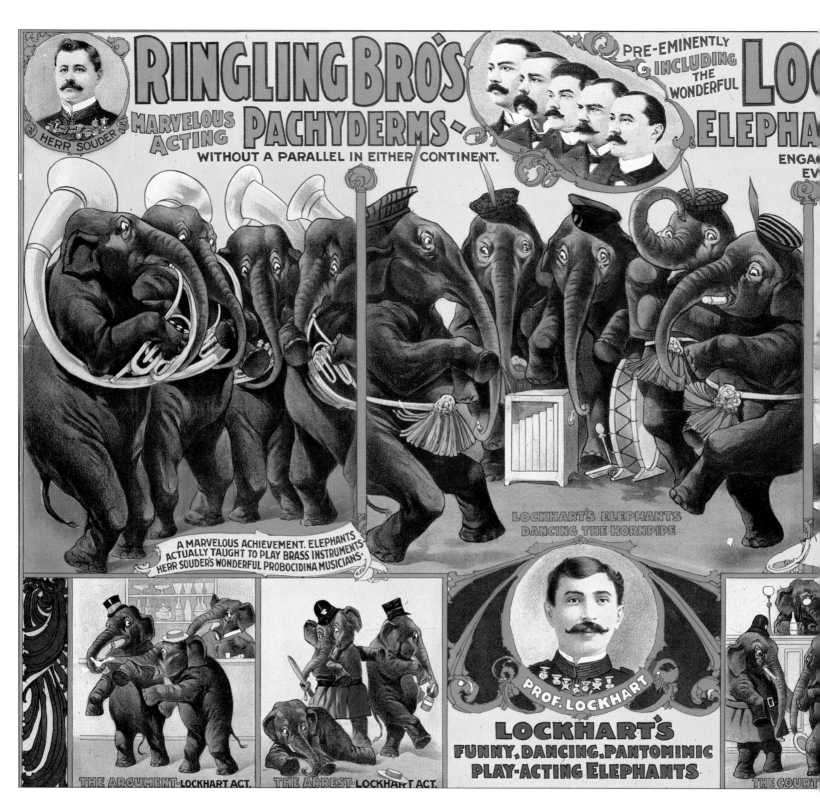

Within the poster image:

RINGLING BROS'

MARVELOUS ACTING PACHYDERMS —

WITHOUT A PARALLEL IN EITHER CONTINENT.

PRE-EMINENTLY INCLUDING THE WONDERFUL LO[...]

ELEPHA[...]

ENGA[...]
EV[...]

HERR SOUDER

A MARVELOUS ACHIEVEMENT. ELEPHANTS ACTUALLY TAUGHT TO PLAY BRASS INSTRUMENTS. HERR SOUDER'S WONDERFUL PROBOCIDINA MUSICIANS.

LOCKHART'S ELEPHANTS DANCING THE HORNPIPE

THE ARGUMENT-LOCKHART ACT.

THE ARREST-LOCKHART ACT.

PROF. LOCKHART

LOCKHART'S FUNNY, DANCING, PANTOMIMIC PLAY-ACTING ELEPHANTS

THE COURT

flowers in a pantomime at the Cirque Olympique in Paris. By the middle of the century individual elephants were delicately stepping over their trainers, standing on their hind legs and doing simple tricks. In 1846 one even walked a double tightrope at Astley's. This was a considerable achievement for the trainer: elephants have an acute sense of balance but are extremely wary of unsteady or unstable surfaces. The same act was achieved in modern times at the Circus Knie in 1941 and again in 1976, but it is much easier to teach elephants to walk along narrow planks or over small areas of support such as a succession of giant bottle shapes.

Elephants have been taught to walk in file, each trunk holding the tail in front, to balance on rolling barrels, and to spin while holding a showgirl in their mouths. In the spectacular 'long mount', the second elephant places its feet on the back of the first and so on down the line. Such a trick as lathering and 'shaving' the

'Professor' Lockhart's elephants. The other trainers probably appeared in the outer rings while he appeared in the centre.

RIGHT, TOP
Franco Knie developed a novel act with elephants and ponies in 1995.

RIGHT, BOTTOM
Billy and Ingrid Wilson Smart and their elephants. Billy is the grandson of British circus owner, the late Billy Smart.

face of a volunteer from the audience used to be a comedy act in Lord George Sanger's and Bertram Mills's circuses and more recently was presented by the Richters and Robert Fossett. However, the most famous elephants only had to be themselves, without performing any tricks at all. Both belonged to P. T. Barnum.

Toung Taloung was the 'Sacred' White Burmese elephant acquired by Barnum in 1884. When it arrived it turned out to be a mottled grey albino and led to one of Forepaugh and Barnum's propaganda battles, and to the expression 'a white elephant', The other was the one and only Jumbo, who added another word to the language. Captured as a baby, he was sold to Paris Zoo, then went to London in exchange for a rhinoceros. He became a favourite of the public at the Zoological Gardens in Regent's Park, and in 17 years thousands of children enjoyed rides on his back. Full grown he was 11 feet (3.3 metres) high and weighed 6.6 tonnes, the biggest

KHART
T COMEDIANS

MONS-JEAN MARCHAND

**AT THE HIGHEST SALARY
PAID ANY ATTRACTION.**

S.MARCHAND'S UNIQUE EXHIBITION
AUGHABLY CLUMSY, PONDEROUS AND
WIELDY HEAVY-WEIGHT BOXERS.

KHART ACT.   THE JAIL-LOCKHART ACT.

elephant known. On reaching breeding age in 1882 he became difficult to handle as he went into musth and was considered unsafe with children. Barnum heard that there was talk of him being destroyed and from across the Atlantic made an offer of $10,000 for him. It was accepted by his owners but when the public found out they were furious. The press, even Queen Victoria and the Prince of Wales objected, but to no avail. Barnum got his elephant and built on the furore to generate the maximum publicity for Jumbo's arrival in America. It cost $20,000 to transport him, but within two weeks of his arrival he had earned more than Barnum's expenses. In six weeks people paid $336,000 to see him!

Jumbo did no tricks but he was the star of the parade, hauled the heaviest equipment and helped raise the big top. In 1885 he was working in a railroad siding at St Thomas, Ontario, unloading for a set-up, when a freight train speeding down an adjoining track struck and

killed him. A little elephant known as Tom Thumb was nearby and Barnum announced that Jumbo had been killed trying to save his tiny friend from injury. He gave Jumbo's skeleton to the Museum of Natural History in New York; the hide was stuffed and sent to Tufts University in Medford, Massachusetts, where it remained until destroyed in a fire in 1975.

Jumbo was an African elephant, few of which were trained before the 1980s when Indian elephants became very hard to buy. Both are now protected by the international convention known as CITES, which forbids export of listed animals, and elephants can now only be shown if captive-bred. Ringling's, whose current star is a male Indian elephant called King Tusk, set up a breeding group in Florida which has so far produced seven calves.

Not only Jumbo but many elephants proved invaluable in pulling wagons, raising tents and drawing crowds to street parades, but most were also trained for the ring. Towards the end of the 19th century Adam Forepaugh Junior became a fine trainer of elephants, though the Forepaugh boxing elephant, presented in 1885, was actually trained by Ephraim Thompson. In the first half of the 20th century elephant trainer Sidney Rink was another of the few blacks to gain some recognition in American circus. George and Sam Lockhart, and the Woodcock family (Babe and Bill, their son William 'Buckles' and his stepson Ben Williams, often with Big Apple Circus) have been outstanding as 20th-century trainers, and Gunther Gebel-Williams showed a wonderful elephant troupe, as well as his big cats (both were taken over on his retirement by his son Mark Oliver Gebel). Fred Logan, once Bill Woodcock's assistant, developed a spectacular walking long mount for the Clyde Beatty-Cole Brothers circus. In Europe post-war troupes have been specially impressive in the Krone, Knie, Billy Smart, Chipperfield and Enis Togni circuses.

The first native American elephant was Columbia, born in the Cooper-Bailey show in 1880. Bailey refused to sell her to Barnum despite an offer of $100,000.

Seals and sealions (often billed as seals) form

another circus tradition, often seen balancing a brightly coloured ball on their snouts. They made only isolated appearances until Joseph Woodward began to show them in the late 19th century. He billed himself as Captain Woodward and wore a naval officer's uniform, which became the customary garb for presenters of seals. His sons developed the act further and in the 1890s were exhibiting six sealions and six seals which caught hats thrown to them and tossed drum-major's batons – even lighted torches – in the air as well as balancing footballs on their snouts.

Recently, the Swiss Gasser family have produced

remarkably complex comedy routines with sealions, which at the end of the act often push their trainer out of the way to take the applause. Roby Gasser has appeared in Las Vegas and with the Big Apple Circus. Her sister Nadia has a separate act.

Large snakes, crocodiles and caymans have sometimes been presented in the ring. The mere sight of their handler working with them provides a thrill. Tahar, with Ringling in the late 1980s, would swim in a tank with an alligator. Other non-performing animals have been a major attraction in the menagerie, especially Gargantua, a gorilla who from 1938 to 1948 was promoted in a similar way to Jumbo half a century earlier. He was an unfortunate animal. In 1931, on the way from Africa, a sailor with a grudge against his owner, the ship's captain, threw acid at the baby gorilla, disfiguring his face. He was bought by Gertrude Lintz, wife of a Brooklyn docker, who nursed him to health and called him Buddha (nickname Buddy) but five years later he was poisoned by a psychotic. He recovered but, perhaps understandably, he now only trusted women and disliked men. He grew too big for Mrs Lintz – the span of his arms was 9 feet (2.7 metres) – and she sold him to Ringling in 1937. Gorillas are not violent creatures unless threatened, but his disfigured appearance made him look very fierce and he drew the public in large numbers, playing a big part in helping Ringling Brothers recover from the setbacks of the Depression.

RIGHT
Adolf, one of Roby Gasser's sealions.
Together, they were winners of a
Gold Clown award at Monte Carlo.

BELOW
Captain Woodward, shown in a
vignette with his sons, and his
sealion act presented by one of them
in 1898.

95

Smaller primates, such as chimpanzees, have proved great performers and dogs have been trained to a range of skills from playing football to substituting for the horses in a chariot race. Rhinoceroses and hippopotami have featured in the ring: Frédy Knie Junior trained a rhino to accept a tiger riding on its back. Troupes of llamas, buffaloes and many more common farm and domestic animals have been presented. Many people consider cats untrainable, but Barnum and Bailey were showing a mixed troupe of cats and pigs in the 1930s and more recently a whole score of cats have been trained by, among others, star Russian clown Yuri Kuklachev, whose cats' tricks include standing on the front paws.

Most surprising, perhaps, of all animal acts was

the appearance in 1985, in the flesh, of entirely mythical animals, in Ringling Brothers ring – unicorns! On close inspection they turned out to be goats but with single, central horns. It would appear, though how is not entirely clear, that the kids' horn buds had been surgically removed and one reset in the central position when they were very young. Kenneth Feld bought all of them for Ringling Brothers to prevent competition, but this echo of Barnum-type 'humbug' is not typical of the modern circus nor its attitude to animals.

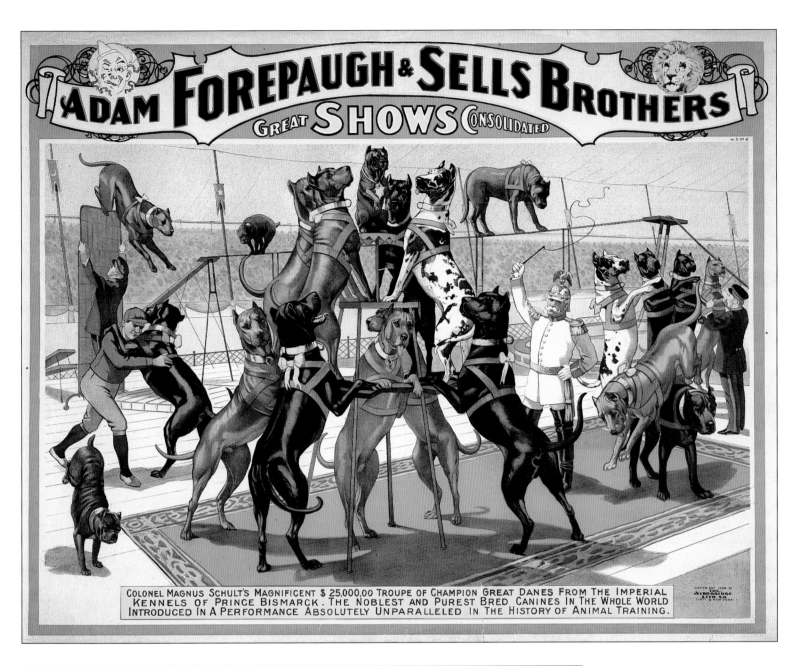

A poster of 1898. Dogs have ben trained to play football or basketball, to pull chariots and, as here, to do a variety of acts that include manoeuvres often seen in displays by police or army dogs.

LEFT
Russian clown Yuri Kuklachev with two of his performing cats.

Mechanized Acts and Daredevils

The original trampoline and the teeter board could send an acrobat some way into the air but in 1871, at the Royal Cremorne Music Hall in London, the trapezist known as Lulu was shot 30 feet (9 metres) upwards where he (for it was actually Eddie Rivers, a young American) grabbed a trapeze bar to end his flight. This feat was achieved by the use of a powerful spring, the patent for which had been taken out by George Farini that year. Six years later, spectators saw a real lady perform a similar feat shot from a cannon. This was Madame Zazel (the very English Miss Napper from Leicester) and the smoke and explosion of the gunpowder were just an effect: propulsion was by a spring. People found the act sensational and others copied it, some using the same name. However, it was dangerous. Miss Napper certainly earned the £20 she was paid for each firing, and she eventually missed the net in which she was supposed to land, broke her back and spent the rest of her life in a steel corset. Some of her imitators were killed.

George Loyal began his cannonball act shortly after and he was appearing with Barnum and Bailey in 1880. He was caught by his wife Ella Zuila, famous for her own high-wire act. They used no net and she hung from a single trapeze high above the launcher, for the trajectory then was almost vertical and the distance travelled short compared with later acts.

While some shot up others plunged down. The German acrobat Ernest Gadbin, billed as Desperado, thrilled audiences before the First World War by swan-diving from a perch 80 feet (24 metres) in the air to land not in water but on a steep ramp. It was polished wood at an angle of 50 degrees inclined down, sprinkled with a layer of cornmeal then curved up from the floor to carry him into the air again to make a final landing in a net. The act had several imitators but they all added protective cushioning to the slide.

In 1922 Hugo Zacchini revived the cannonball act, first in Malta with his father Ildebrando's Zacchini Brothers Circus, and it became his family's speciality. He was seen by John Ringling in Copenhagen and presented in America by him in 1929. The Zacchinis were copied by the Leinerts in Germany. These acts used compressed air, not a spring, and said they could make their 'human bullet' travel 200 feet (60 metres), though the *Guinness Book of Records* (1997) gave the greatest distance as 180 feet (55 metres) by David Smith in New Jersey in 1995. In 1934 Hugo Zacchini and his brother Victor added a variation by being shot simultaneously on the Ringling show. Such acts continue, though today they are more likely to be rockets than cannonballs!

A similar act is the Human Arrow. Its first performer was Tony Zedoras, billed as Alar, in Barnum and Bailey's Circus in 1896. The present record distance for the act is held by Ariana (the Bulgarian Vesta Gueschkova) at Ringling Brothers and Barnum and Bailey at Tampa, Florida, in 1995.

The invention of the bicycle was exploited on the

wire and in trick riding around the ring. There were already cycling acts in the days of the penny-farthing, and not only on the flat. A 'Bicycle Circus' was exhibited in London's Agricultural Hall as early as 1869. Beginning with displays of 'wheelsmanship' there were soon elaborate balancing acts, in which the Chinese have since become specialists, achieving a record 14 girls on one bicycle in a current display.

When the velocipede and high-wheel performers disappeared, Nick Kaufman, from Rochester, New York, became the doyen of trick riders, beating Feliz Brunner in competition in 1900. Brunner's son 'Artix,' with partner Rodella Ruis, did jumps and somersaults over the handlebars on polished-nickel cycles with wheels slightly closer than standard models but otherwise identical. Arthur Klein, in grotesque clown outfit, would ride out on a tiny cycle 12 inches (30 cm) high to join his family cycle troupe, returning on successively larger models until his final entrance on a motorbike that exploded under him. The Chinese circus has produced cycle acts that feature multiple riders and leaps from cycle to cycle.

Both low and high unicycle riding have become standard circus skills but few can match such teams as the King Charles troupe, one of the first big modern African-American acts, when they appeared with Ringlings from 1969 in their unicycle basketball game.

In 1883 Frenchman Leonati, the 'Spiral Ascensionist', was cycling up and down a spiral on a penny-farthing for Forepaugh and in 1902 Forepaugh-Sells had a similar ascensionist on a unicycle negotiating a spiral only 10 inches (25 cm) wide and going 60 feet (18 metres) high. The following year the monosyllabic Starr, on an ordinary bicycle, sped down from the top of a 79-foot (23.7-metres) ladder angled at 52 degrees, gaining enough momentum to freewheel right round the hippodrome track that circled the rings, while Kilpatrick claimed a descent of 100 feet (30 metres) down a flight of steps. Earlier, in 1899, Mlle Zizi had thrilled American crowds by cycling on air, launching herself from a track to clear six elephants without support in an outdoor attraction with the Walter Main Circus, while in another cycling act Diavolo whirled around a track to loop the loop.

With the development of the motorcycle such acts could add the machismo of the revving up and roar of engines and the extra speed. The thrill of the motorbike

led to the creation of the cage-like 'Globe of Death' inside which bikers circled round and round and upside down, crossing and recrossing each other's path. In more recent times the motorbike became a central image in the creation of the tradition-breaking French circus Archaos.

The automobile in its turn was used in such daredevil acts. The tracks for these were more easily erected out of doors so that they were often an added attraction to bring audiences to the circus rather than being presented in the ring. Mlle Mauricia de Tiers, billed as 'the Fearless, Young and Fascinating Parisian', made a car leap upside-down for Barnum and Bailey in 1905. Two years later an American woman, Isabella Butler, was

Diavolo (G. Fred Matthiessen) speeds down a ramp to loop the loop.

doing a similar act for them.

An announcement made in connection with the appearance of Octavie la Tour in New York with her similar Le Tourbillon de la Mort (Whirlwind of Death) in 1905 could be applied not only to such daredevil stunts but to many other circus acts:

'The trouble is not in finding people with courage to perform the feats, but in working out a stunt more terrible than anything ventured before, that will menace life and all but take it. For hairbreadth as the escape must seem, the probability of accident must be really small. No one wants to see people die. The fame is one of mettle, not of death.'

LEFT
The Czech Faltiny Family form a unicycle carousel for a balancing act.

RIGHT
The Space Wheel, with the Italian Circo Medrano of the Casartelli family. This apparatus, sometimes known as the Wheel of Death and first used in the 1970s by the Sensational Leighs, is now one of the mostly widely seen new circus routines. As it turns the artists skip, handstand, juggle and jump while on the two wheels. The faster the wheel turns the more spectacular (and dangerous) it becomes.

OPPOSITE
A poster of 1900. Note that one of Kilpatrick's legs has been amputated but he still performed his feat on an ordinary bicycle.

THREE
A New Golden Age

Many people look back on the circus of the past as a lost Golden Age, and it is true that mid and late 20th-century circus has faced many problems. But circus life was never easy and today circus not only survives but flourishes. There is a new interest in circus skills and new kinds of circus are developing. It is a different world with different audiences but the excitement, humour and spectacular thrills continue undiminished.

The Knie Big Top in Geneva.

Post-War Problems

During the Second World War the United States government encouraged circus as a useful element in maintaining people's spirits, but in Europe circuses, if they continued to operate, faced enormous problems, not only because artists were called up for military service, tents and transport requisitioned, and vital supplies unobtainable, but from authorities' reluctance to allow circuses to perform in cities where bombing might leave dangerous and perhaps wounded animals roaming their streets. But the show still went on. In England, for instance, the permanent Tower Circus in Blackpool and the touring Sir Robert Fossett Circus were among those that kept going. The Bouglione Brothers and Amar circuses survived the war in France, where German enthusiasm for circus seems to have afforded them a more lenient time during the Occupation. However, the war forced many circuses to close and stopped the constant travel from country to country that refreshes circus productions.

Even in the United States wartime shortages had their effect, most dramatically in 1944 at Hartford, Connecticut, where Ringling was playing in a tent which, through scarcity of materials, had not been rendered flameproof. At a crowded matinée performance fire broke out and rapidly spread through the big top. In six minutes 168 people were left dead and 487 injured: burned, smothered or crushed in the rush to get to the exits, two of which were blocked by animal tunnels set for Alfred Court's big cats and bears (though seven were clear). In the panic no one thought of simply lifting the side walls of the tent and ducking beneath them. A month later the circus was back on the road under new canvas, but it took ten years to pay off the $4.5 million compensation claims.

Immediately after the war, as new circuses were formed and old ones rebuilt, all forms of entertainment, especially circuses, enjoyed a boom, but in the 1950s and early '60s they found that they were facing increasing competition for audiences. There were many new demands on people's leisure time, especially television, which kept people at home. Appearances on television created new opportunities for circus artists and could be

The colourful flags flying high above the brightly painted midway of the Clyde Beatty-Cole Brothers Circus, a thriving tented American touring company.

good publicity but did not necessarily help sell tickets to see live an act already shown on TV.

By 1955 Ringling Brothers and Barnum and Bailey were grossing $5 million but losing $1 million. John Ringling North decided that the tenting show had to end. In future their circuses would appear only in big arenas. In *The Circus Kings: Our Ringling Family Story*, he reasoned that audiences were failing because:

'They simply could not get there. It took a fifteen-acre lot to hold the forty-one tents in which the circus lived and showed. And you needed another big lot to park three thousand cars. With suburbs ringing every city in America from three to thirty miles in depth where on earth could you still find a fifteen acre lot that could be reached by public transportation or even conveniently by automobile? The answer was virtually nowhere. Thus we had been gradually pushed farther and farther from the urban centres until we were practically pitching our tents in the sticks. It was not the American people forsaking us. We had forsaken them.'

The change to big indoor locations proved successful and, especially after the purchase of the show by Irvin Feld in 1967 and its subsequent management by him and his son Kenneth, it has gone from strength to strength.

Small tenting circuses touring away from the big centres may not have had Ringling's difficulties over sites but found it increasingly hard to offer an entertainment that matched expectations created by other media on the ticket-sales which such enterprises could attract. The one-ring European circuses may not have had the problems of scale either but other pressures applied and, worldwide, some circuses fell by the wayside. Circus people had faced tough times before and many circuses survived, sometimes using pop stars to front their shows and other devices to attract a new audience. Management problems did not stop artists from developing new acts and in some cases surpassing the skills of their predecessors.

In Britain the great Bertram Mills Circus closed its tenting show at the end of the 1964 season, Cyril Mills believing that increasing prices to match costs would exclude the family audiences for which they catered. After a successful final London season at Olympia in 1965-56 the circus was sold, and it played only one more season, under the ownership of Maxwell Joseph. The Chipperfields' family circus, which had grown to be the biggest in Europe in 1953-55, left for South Africa ten years later, though it returned in 1969 and is still going strong. Billy Smart's, begun in 1946 by a former funfair proprietor, grew to be a major circus but stopped tenting in 1971 and, after presenting a number of annual television shows, eventually closed. In 1993 it recommenced operation with autumn seasons only.

But new circuses started too: Gerry Cottle's, for instance, and later a circus started by his daughters. Mary Chipperfield and other members of her family ran their own shows after her father Jimmy had developed the first safari park at Longleat, Wiltshire, where visitors in cars or special minibuses drive through a landscape with big cats and other wild life roaming uncaged. In the 1970s and '80s, Hoffman, Robert Brothers, Sir Robert Fossett and Austen Brothers ran circuses similar in size to Cottle's and Chipperfield's.

A similar story can be told elsewhere. Only the state circuses of the USSR, China and Eastern Europe seemed unchallenged by economics and changing public taste – their problems were to come with the political changes of the late 1980s. Geography, national attitudes and the adaptability of proprietors helped to ensure the success of circuses in many places.

In Scandinavia the original Cirkus Schumann closed down in 1969, but circus remains popular in Denmark, with Cirkus Benneweis continuing its long tradition, and in Sweden and in Norway, where Knut Dahl has established Circus Merano as one of Europe's finest shows. Circuses large and small flourish in Switzerland, headed by Circus Knie, the world's finest one-ring circus, and recently Louis Knie has taken over the National Circus in neighbouring Austria. Germany still has upwards of 100 touring circuses and, while some great names of the past such as Karl Hagenbeck and Franz Althoff are no longer travelling, there remains Krone, with a vast tenting show and permanent building in Munich, Circus Barum, owned by wild-animal trainer Gerd Siemoneit, and Bernard Paul's Circus Roncalli, with a cult following in the major cities. Italy has over 300 circuses, from small ones to giants like those of Moira Orfei, Enis Togni and Liana Orfei, and Spain has a good number too, led by Circo Mondial. In France the well-established names such as Pinder and Amart have been bought and leased by new promoters: in one season an amazing 26 circuses named Bouglione were travelling! The French Gruss family has risen to new heights with Alexis Gruss's Cirque à l'Ancienne, which plays seasons in Paris and at a château in Orange, and his cousin Arlette Gruss formed what is currently the best touring circus, produced by her son Gilbert. In Australia, Ashton's Circus has recently been joined by new shows, including proprietors from Europe, and in South Africa the Boswell Wilkie Circus, now in its fifth decade, has continued to entertain in the post-apartheid era.

In America Ringling's tours two units and has sent a third abroad, Carson and Barnes and Circus Vargas are still going strong, as well as many smaller shows and the new types of circus described below.

In recent years circus has also had to face another challenge. Growing awareness of the damage which human exploitation has inflicted upon the natural world and an active concern for the conservation and care of animals brought criticism of animal acts as cruel and unethical.

Such criticism was not entirely new. Animal-welfare societies had long ago protested at cruelty in animal training and the conditions in which animals were kept. But from the days of Karl Hagenbeck such things began to change. Of course, there will be exceptions, who deserve the worst the law can inflict, but circus folk would be the first to agree on strict regulation of standards of animal welfare. Not only do they care for their animals but they depend upon them for their livelihood. It is a matter of economics as well as sentiment that they be kept happy and healthy, both physically and psychologically, and there is no question that the stimulation of contact and performance is better than the boredom that creates so many problems for animals in a zoo. Most people today would also argue against the capture of wild animals, for zoos or for circuses, except to provide a breeding pool to prevent

The finale of the Circus World Championships. Held eleven times (1976-86), usually in London but shown worldwide on television, the championships were the idea of three men: Adrian Metcalfe, silver-medal winner at the 1964 Olympics and now television commentator and producer, Ivor David Balding, the American who went on to found Circus Flora, and television sports producer Tony McCarthy. Like the Circus Festival held each year at Monte Carlo, they brought an element of competition to the circus world and encouraged a more informed circus public: people saw and compared the best acrobats and aerialists from Europe, North America, Russia and China. Festivals and competitions raise standards and act as showcases for new talent. Many agents and circus directors attend, looking for new acts.

extinction. Such sentiments inevitably led to fewer animals in the ring. But circus acts also attract criticism from those who believe that training any animals to perform is unacceptable exploitation. Their arguments may be equally applied to those who use horses for haulage or to ride, race dogs, or by extension keep pets of any kind.

Such concern has led to legislation in Sweden, where a law passed as early as 1960 bans the appearance of most wild animals in circuses, permitting only those that are seen as not being humiliated or degraded by training – horses, asses, zebras, camels, llamas, goats, pigs, dogs, cats, sealions, doves and parrots – and there are restrictions in other Scandinavian countries. In Britain some local authorities refuse to let sites formerly used by touring circuses to any which present animal acts, though the legal validity of this has been challenged and there is nothing to stop circuses with animals appearing on privately owned land. In 1980 the American Society for the Prevention of Cruelty to Animals and various animal-rights groups began to raise opposition, and the town of Hollywood, Florida, passed legislation in 1991 prohibiting the display for entertainment of any 'vertebrate animals' (though presumably making an exception of humans) on property owned by or leased from the city.

In Britain the Royal Society for the Prevention of Cruelty to Animals is strongly against animals in circuses and commissioned an independent scientific report from animal-behaviour expert Marthe Kiley-Worthington. She concluded that there was no evidence of cruelty during training or transportation of circus animals, that training was professionally done and generally of a high standard, and that welfare of animals judged on physical and psychological criteria was not inferior to that of other animal husbandry in zoos, stables and kennels. She recommended that more training should take place, so that animals learn new things all the time, and that more weight should be given to performances that emphasize the animals' inherent characteristics. She found that certain housing conditions severely restricted the animals' behaviour and recommended that lions and tigers should have access to built-up exercise areas as well as the wagons they regard as their dens for eating and sleeping, and that elephants should not be chained by the foot but allowed to exercise in areas enclosed by electric fencing.

British circuses, and reputable ones elsewhere, responded positively to her findings by the provision of such exercise areas, though there are still some around the world that have not implemented them. At Ringling's each trainer and groom is given a copy of her book *Animals in Circuses and Zoos: Chiron's World?* to study. Although many trainers tend to stick with routines that have been successful in the past rather than invent new ones, some progress has been made in that direction, and in British circuses trainers and keepers are on hand when audiences, fascinated to learn at first hand about the animals, visit them after the show. The Association of Circus Proprietors in Britain has drawn up its own stringent code of conduct for animal welfare.

Most circus goers still see animal acts as an integral part of circus, but those who object to the use of animals can now find circuses without them. Their growth probably owes as much to the burgeoning of interest in circus skills as to ethical considerations, but some circuses have stopped showing animals in response to popular opinion or legislation.

Back in 1925 John Ringling dropped big-cat acts from his show, announcing that he felt the public did not want to see them. However, he kept other animal acts and soon brought the big cats back again. In Britain the Blackpool Tower has banned animal acts, and Peter Jay, who had held the contract to provide the circus there for several years, has transferred his show to the local pleasure beach.

The New Circus

From this scene, in which motorbikes reared up like circus horses and leaped over a white Mercedes, Archaos's first production climaxed in an anarchic finale with a fiddling violinist on a bike being hauled up by its rear wheel to the top of the tent, while parts of the rigging collapsed around him in general smoke and mayhem, to a backing of frenzied rock music .

*TOP
A programme for Le Cirque National which Alexis Gruss presented in a show inspired by the circus paintings of Picasso and Lautrec.*

*LEFT
Mast acrobatics in Cirque du Soleil's Saltimbanco.*

Circus on the pattern of the multi-ring circuses of the past continues in North America: in the 1990s Carson and Barnes presented five rings of continuous action. But new companies have sprung up which adopt a different approach and established companies have changed their style to accommodate new attitudes and to appeal more to contemporary tastes.

In the 1960s the development of a flourishing street life for entertainers led to a renewed interest in circus skills. The barriers between entertainment forms were falling. Actors and dancers sometimes learned balancing, juggling and other disciplines, fine-arts exponents began to take in performance art and circus people were influenced by new ideas about performance. Some of the new practitioners found themselves jobs in existing circus. Some came together to create their own shows. In Australia, for instance, a group of acrobats and musicians formed a collective in the 1970s to create the cabaret Circus Oz, Australia's official representative at the cultural Olympiad at the 1984 Los Angeles Olympics. Later, a group of 50 Australian youngsters aged seven upwards, who had learned their circus skills in Albury-Wodonga, formed another company, the Flying Fruit Fly Circus. Neither circus had animal acts.

In France Jean-Baptiste Thierrée, a circus artist from his teens who had subsequently become an actor, and Victoria Chaplin, with father Charlie's clowning tradition in her blood, founded *Le Cirque Bonjour*. It was launched at the Avignon Festival in 1971 with over 30 artists and animals including elephants and big cats, but with a theatrical sensibility in its presentation. Over the years they reduced their numbers and adopted a more intimate scale with *Le Cirque Imaginaire*, in which rabbits and other small creatures featured, until today they have a show without any animals which has abandoned most of the trappings of circus to present what they consider a 'distillation of the memory of circus' in their current show *Le Cercle Invisible* (The Invisible Circle). It really owes more to their imaginative performance skills than to conventional circus.

In contrast, but also from France, came the Archaos Cirque de Caractère, founded in 1986 by Pierrot Pillot-Bidon and later given support by the French government. This is the 'heavy metal' of circus, often quite literally, as its clowns carry sheets of corrugated iron on their backs. Blasting rock music, motorbikes, chain-saws, nudity and violence in a circus ring polarized

BELOW RIGHT
A handbill for the French circus troupe Archaos Cirque de Caractère in their 1995/6 show Game Over.

BELOW LEFT
Jean-Baptiste Thierrée in Le Cercle Invisible. *The theatrical trick of exploiting a dummy to create a duo was employed by the comic riders of the early circus.*

reaction. It outraged some and in Britain attempts were made to ban performances, but it found an enthusiastic audience and grew in size, producing a succession of staggering shows. Despite a reputation for being bad and dangerous it also displayed whimsical Gallic charm, romantic trapeze work and ballets on bicycles besides breathtakingly dangerous globes of death and at some performances juggling with chain-saws. Creator Pillot-Bidon saw his work quite differently from the way his critics did, declaring in the *Guardian* newspaper, when the show was performing in Britain in 1990, that 'there is no vulgarity, no outrageous sex scenes, no dangerous aggression, only sensuality, violence and enormous tenderness, as there is in life.' At its peak Archaos was running a television company, a set builder and a circus school as well as touring two shows. In 1992 its tent blew away in Dublin and the company went bankrupt, only to be swiftly reborn. Performances grew to stadium size and the 1995 show *Game Over* was specifically designed for large, rock-music venues.

Although not always apparent to the audience there was a message and story line to the performances of the 1990s. *Metal Clown* (1991), for example, was announced as 'a vivid deconstruction of the culture clash between the European invaders of South America and its indigenous peoples'. The clowns became the conquistadors, with the

THE SOUTH BANK CENTRE IN ASSOCIATION WITH ICA PRESENT

FLYING FRUIT FLY CIRCUS

FROM AUSTRALIA

ORDINARY KIDS DOING EXTRAORDINARY THINGS

MAY 22-MAY 31
JUBILEE GARDENS
(NEXT TO ROYAL FESTIVAL HALL)

SUN 22
MON 23-FRI 27   4.30 pm
SAT 28   7.30 pm
NO PERFORMANCE SUNDAY MAY 29
BANK HOLIDAY—   2.30 pm & 7.30 pm
MON 30
TUES 31   2.30 pm & 7.30 pm
                 7.30 pm

TICKETS £6
£4 (18 & UNDER, STUDENTS, UB40,
SENIOR CITIZENS)
ADVANCE TICKETS AVAILABLE FROM ROYAL
FESTIVAL HALL BOX OFFICE 10 am TO 9 pm
TEL 01-928 3191 CREDIT CARDS 01-928 8800
TICKETS ON THE NIGHT AVAILABLE ONLY FROM
JUBILEE GARDENS BOX OFFICE FROM 5.30 pm.

G. Martin.

THE SOUTH BANK CENTRE

Arts Council Funded

Brazilian dance troupe Bahia Axe Bahia representing the
Native Americans. *Game Over* presented a Genet-like
post-holocaust world under a fascist dictator, but with
traditional circus skills clearly apparent and much more
dominant than the narrative.

Archaos have had a direct effect on some other
circuses. In 1995, for instance, Pierrot Pillot-Bidon helped
Gerry Cottle devise a new presentation for his British
circus with *Circus of Horrors*.

Even the Russian circus found a need for change.
Valentin Kuznetsov, director of the Leningrad Circus,
declared in 1987: *'Technical skill alone is a thing of the
past. The overriding aim is now to communicate an
emotion to the audience. In the Soviet Union today, a
circus performance is planned as if it were a piece of
drama with a prologue, action and epilogue...but the
progression must be sustained by a heightening of
emotion. This is where the* entrée *clown, typical of the
USSR, comes in. The whole programme hinges on him, he
is the hub of the action.'*

*Flying Fruit Fly Circus – 'ordinary
kids doing extraordinary things' –
was a once-off 1980 company but
there have been longer-lived youth
and student circuses in the United
States, run for their educational
and social value.*

The epitome of the theatrical in circus is to be seen
in the productions of the Cirque du Soleil. This Canadian
company was created by stilt-walker, juggler and
magician Guy Laliberté together with former actor Guy
Caron, a clown who had already started a circus school in
Montreal. It had its origins in a group of street performers
whom he formed into a company for an entertainers'
festival at Baie-Saint-Paul, Quebec, in 1982: the Club des
talons hauts (High-heels Club). In 1984, with the
assistance of the Quebec government, they put on a show
as part of the celebration of the 450th anniversary of
Jacques Cartier's arrival in Canada. It mixed circus arts
and street theatre with wildly outrageous costumes, all set
to specially composed music and magically lit – lighting
has been an important element in all their shows. They
opened in an 800-seat tent in Gaspé, toured ten other
towns in Quebec and the next year were in Ontario and
Vancouver, as well as sending individual acts to various
festivals. Next year a new show, *Cirque Réinventé*, went
to the Los Angeles Festival and subsequently toured the

enhanced by classical music and including students from the circus school which Gruss established with the help of Sylvia Monfort. It has always been particularly strong in equestrian skills, with liberty and *haute école* horses. Typical themes of their shows have celebrated painters of the circus, or circus films, and From Paris to Peking was shaped to feature artists from China.

The Cirque à l'Ancienne was acknowledged as an influence by Paul Binder who, in the Big Apple Circus in New York, created the first of the new American circuses, abandoning the huge arenas and multi-rings and adopting the single ring, with a more European approach and an intimate ambience.

Binder worked first as a television stage manager, then took a business course but, following the break-up of his first marriage, became a juggler with a mime troupe in San Francisco. That led to a trip to Europe where he and companion Michael Christensen (later juggler and clown with Big Apple) hoped to survive as street entertainers. In Paris they were offered jobs with Annie Fratellini's Nouveau Cirque, and when Binder returned to New York it became his dream to restore circus the way it used to be. Researching old prints and records he came to feel that '*the classical circus had been lost in this country as early as the 1830s, when theatricality and poetry began to give way to daredevilry and menageries, when artistry began to give way to commercialism.*' If it had not, perhaps there would never have been any of the typical big American circuses, and Binder felt that the kind of intimate circus he wanted would not be a commercial proposition in America, so he set out to find backing for a one-ring circus.

United States, London and Paris while another show opened in Montreal in a new and bigger tent. That travelled to Tokyo and a tour of Japan and more productions followed. Now Soleil have a production office in Amsterdam as well as Canada. A venue specially built for them in Las Vegas will be opening in 1998, which will give them two shows running in Las Vegas. Another theatre is being built for them in Berlin and still more venues are planned. Meanwhile, their ninth production, premiered in Canada in 1996, is touring for three years in America before it goes abroad.

They have come a long way from street theatre. Some shows are extremely extravagant, costumes alone have cost an average of $3,000 each and have gone as high as $420,000. *Quidam*, the 1996 production, had an elaborate aluminium set with overhead tracks carrying computer-controlled trolleys to place equipment, props and performers in position. Rehearsal and development is intensive: for this show the troupe rehearsed for a whole year developing conceptually new acrobatic numbers and an aerial ballet. The investment is prodigious in both effort and money and only their worldwide success has made such shows possible. Each show has a definite theme which is carried through in costuming and presentation, though the individual acts still feature traditional circus skills.

The themed circus had an earlier manifestation in the Circus Roncalli, which Bernhard Paul and André Heller assembled in Vienna in 1976. Paul's vision was to created a 'poetic circus' and he produced what can be called total environment. His softly lit blue and red tent was approached through a group of art-nouveau caravans with wrought-iron railings and leaded windows. Spectators entered the tent beneath a sign inviting each to 'be a poet' and as they passed they were showered with confetti snow and greeted by clowns, some being embraced or having hearts or stars painted upon their cheeks. A beautiful young man, the 'Angel of Possible Miracles', fulfilled the role of ringmaster and among the acts were three gold-painted men performing a sensual adagio, a balletic adaptation of the living statues of years before. Circus Roncalli performances are now rather more conventional, but that original style was taken up by the National Youth Circus created by Gerry Cottle in Britain, which toured in 1984-85, and has certainly influenced others.

Another European circus, the Cirque à l'Ancienne, also gives each show a theme. Started in 1974 by Alexis Gruss with his father, clown Dede, wife Gypsy Bouglione, brother Patrick and sister Martine, it returned to circus roots, aiming at artistic quality with routines

Kristalleon (Christopher Miller) from Germany and Tunga (Tungalag Has-Ochyrin) from Mongolia in Big Apple Circus's Going Places *(1992).*

Big Apple Circus staged its 1996 show as though set in a small town at the turn of the century. Doc Pitcham's wonder elixir produces amazing reactions, thrills and laughter from acrobats, aerialists, performing dogs, clowns and circus animals.

He got enough support to be able to present a show consisting of ten acts in Battery Park, New York, in 1971 and subsequently developed an audience in many cities, including Boston, Philadelphia, Pittsburgh and Washington, D.C., as well as taking a regular tented pitch at Lincoln Center in New York. He managed to attract many top names in international circus, most notably one of the world's great equestriennes, Katja Schumann of the Copenhagen circus family, who later became his wife. Big Apple has created its own stars too, such as the Back Street Flyers tumbling troupe who trained at their own circus school.

With the Big Apple, too, each season's show is themed, though conducted by a ringmaster who originally was Paul himself. One year he took the theme of Coney Island, another the world's great carnivals, conjuring up Venice and Mardi Gras in New Orleans. The whole company danced in a Mexican fiesta while the ring was rigged for the Flying Goanas, for whose act the company became part of the audience – typical of the continuous linking of the show. In 1996 it was the Medicine Show, set in a country town a century ago and revolving around the visit of the medicine man Doc Pitcham.

On the West Coast the first of the new circuses was the Pickle Family Circus, based on San Francisco. Founded initially in 1974 as the Pickle Family Jugglers by Peggy Snider and Larry Pisoni (who had met as members of the San Franciso Mime Troupe), it was expanded into a circus which put emphasis on the skill of the performer rather than daredevilry, did not feature animals, and was one of the first to use completely modern music, jazz in style and specially written for each act. It was run as a cooperative and everybody shared in set-ups and tear-downs, with performances either in indoor auditoria or outdoors surrounded by a tenting sidewall, but never in a tent. A circus school was opened in 1984. Originally presented as a traditional succession of separate acts, by

Cirque du Soleil make spectacular use of costume, lighting and theatrical expertise to create an exciting ambience for their productions.

An aerial ballet on bungee lines in Cirque du Soleil's Saltimbanco.

1990 the style was being structured more theatrically – a cause of dissension when founder Pisoni returned to the company after a break working elsewhere. Snider also resigned in 1991 and the company went bankrupt in 1993. Though they did not survive, they helped develop many artists and made an important contribution to the pattern of change, influencing the Cirque du Soleil which in turn influenced them.

In 1985 came Circus Flora, founded by David Balding, Sam and Sheila Balding, Jewell and Sacha Pavalata as an educational nonprofit-making corporation, which tours the Midwest from its base in St Louis. It too is a one-ring circus, presenting a show linked by a story line.

Such shows as these have set a pattern for others which have joined the remaining established circuses. Though Paul Binder found his inspiration in the past, neither his nor the other new circuses are really like the old ones. They are circuses of our own time, reflecting contemporary taste, just as Barnum's humbug echoed the wheeling and dealing of the gilded age. With animals or without, modern circus can offer amazing acts and fantastic shows. Competition at the many circus festivals around the world, headed by the annual Circus Festival in Monte Carlo and the Cirque de Demain in Paris which presents up and coming artists, show that today's performers maintain the skill and dedication of their forebears, and sometimes excel them. If the clock has come full circle it is in the rediscovery of grace and artistry in circus presentation. The rope dancer, the equestrian ballerina and perhaps the storytelling of the Tailor's Ride to Brentford are the prototypes that are reflected in the 'new' circus. If it can offer not just the thrills and amazement of acrobatic and other physical skills but a complete and satisfying emotional experience, there surely is a new golden age ahead – and one which has a place for every size of show from 'The Greatest Show on Earth' to *Le Cercle Invisible.*

'What do you say to the public at the end of the show?'
'What do you say to the public, my dear Mimile? You say goodbye of course!'
'WRONG Boullicot! You never say goodbye to the public, you say: Here's to the next time!'
Closing dialogue between French clowns Emile Recordier (1890-1946) and Alphonse Boullicot (1878-1957)

INDEX

Page numbers in *italics* refer to illustrations

B